THE SOUL'S JOURNEY

Reflections on
The Interior Castle [St Teresa of Avila]

Patricia Greene PhD

Copyright © 2015 Patricia Greene PhD.

All rights reserved. No part of this book may be used or reproduced by any means, graphic, electronic, or mechanical, including photocopying, recording, taping or by any information storage retrieval system without the written permission of the publisher except in the case of brief quotations embodied in critical articles and reviews.

Balboa Press books may be ordered through booksellers or by contacting:

Balboa Press
A Division of Hay House
1663 Liberty Drive
Bloomington, IN 47403
www.balboapress.com.au
1 (877) 407-4847

Because of the dynamic nature of the Internet, any web addresses or links contained in this book may have changed since publication and may no longer be valid. The views expressed in this work are solely those of the author and do not necessarily reflect the views of the publisher, and the publisher hereby disclaims any responsibility for them.

The author of this book does not dispense medical advice or prescribe the use of any technique as a form of treatment for physical, emotional, or medical problems without the advice of a physician, either directly or indirectly. The intent of the author is only to offer information of a general nature to help you in your quest for emotional and spiritual well-being. In the event you use any of the information in this book for yourself, which is your constitutional right, the author and the publisher assume no responsibility for your actions.

Any people depicted in stock imagery provided by Thinkstock are models, and such images are being used for illustrative purposes only.
Certain stock imagery © Thinkstock.

The scriptural quotations are from The New Revised Standard Version copyright @1989, by the Division of Christian Education of the Council of Education of the National Council of The Churches of Christ in the U.S.A. and are used by permission. All rights reserved.

Print information available on the last page.

ISBN: 978-1-4525-2802-1 (sc)
ISBN: 978-1-4525-2803-8 (e)

Balboa Press rev. date: 06/12/2015

Celebrating 500 years

St Teresa of Avila 1515-2015

With John of the Cross, Teresa established the first convent of Discalced Carmelites. Teresa went on to found throughout Spain, seventeen convents under the spiritual guidance of John of the Cross. Teresa was conferred *Doctor Ecclesiae* by the University of Salamanca in 1617. In 1970 Pope Paul VI conferred on her, the honour of Doctor of the Church.

Profit from the sale of this book will be divided and donated to;

Save the Children
&
The Malala Fund

Contents

Acknowledgements ix
Introduction xvii

Part 1: Obstacles to Soul Growth 1
    The spiritual journey

Part 2: The awakened soul 9
    Mansions One 15
    Reflection 22

    Mansions Two 27
    Reflection 32

Part 3: Purifying the senses 37
    Mansions Three 43
    Reflection 49

    Mansions Four 55
    Reflection 60

Part 4: Your quest for holiness –Tsedeq 65
    Mansions Five 73
    Reflection 79

Mansions Six 85
Reflection 91

Mansions Seven 97
Reflection 103

Bibliography 109
Appendix 1: Lectio Divina (Guigo 11) 111
Epilogue 113
About the author 115

Acknowledgements

Soul journeying is difficult – it involves pain and confrontation

A difficult passage for me began in 2010 after a workplace crisis in the previous year. Months later, there was the accompaniment of devastation as my career, after 43 years of service of care to others was ended. I am grateful for those who walked beside me at different stages of that journey;

Marie Cheeseman, Sr Josephine Dillon RSM and Rita Murphy.

In a year of transitions I relocated from Perth to NSW to be closer to family. My dear doctoral supervisor at Curtin University waited patiently for the final thesis write up, that required I focus at a high level of analytic coherency. It was accomplished despite my struggles with rawness and pain, compounded with financial difficulty too! This book is the by-product of that time.

At that time, my daily routine was to walk by the sea at Umina, after which the thesis was written into the fullness of each day. A daily spiritual workout, focused on *forgiveness* with self reflection and visits back and forth to rooms in the first mansions of my soul. Like the floods that had devastated Queensland in that year, I too attended a massive clean up of the debris of distress. Instead of being twisted and hard hearted, I wished to become a *'whole person'* in my journey into older age. Then aha! There was a break through instead of a break down, and also my anthropology thesis was well received in 2011. In that year I returned to Perth to face the tiger, being metaphorically my fear.

When this manuscript was first conceived in 2013, delays fortuitously occurred, as not until September 2014 did I glean a new perspective on the importance of forgiveness. It came from a program through the Monastery of the Heart (MOH) when Sr. Joan Chittister, OSB, presented a webinar on; God's Tender Mercy: Reflections on Forgiveness. A wonderful gift for many people, which would have assisted others like me. With heartfelt gratefulness for the program and for that revelation, *thank you Sr. Joan and the Benedictine Sisters of Lake Erie Pennsylvania, USA, and also MOH members.*

Forgiveness is essential for all of human life
if we desire a world of peace

Thank you also to Father Jerome Watt O. Carm who gave encouragement after reading the first daft and referred me to Father Greg Burke (OCD – Discalced Carmelites) who after he had read the draft made comments for improvement and said, "…it will help many people".

Thanks to Vivienne Litson who reviewed my introduction of a later draft and also to Ruth Dreaver.

Not least, my feline friend 'Rosie', who awakens me early to seek God, often too early!

Dedication

To two great spiritual midwives who have helped birth my soul;

Teresa of Avila

&

Rita Murphy

A former spiritual adviser of Ain Karim Bridgetown
who has been a spiritual midwife for many
a soul over the past decades.

In the growth of our soul's formation on our spiritual journey – *humility is paramount*. Chapter 7 in The Rule of Benedict, divides humility into 12 steps, of which step 3 is to be obedient to one's superior. It may be put like this, for *one to have the preparedness to listen to the one wiser than oneself*. To grow inwardly, we need to be open to hear what others have to say, who have thus journeyed far ahead of us, and who now support us on our journey, with good advice that hastens our soul growth.

Foreword

It is with joy that I welcome Patricia Greene's *The Soul's Journey*. Patricia gives us a practical guide to living the timeless message of St Teresa's *Interior Castle*. This book brings the wisdom of St Teresa to people today in a helpful and accessible manner.

As it happens in 2015, the fifth centenary of her birth, we have joyfully celebrated the gift of St Teresa of Ávila. She was a woman who is still a source of inspiration and wisdom 500 years after her birth on 28 March 1515. She was original, courageous and determined as well as intelligent, charming and witty. She battled entrenched racism and misogyny in both church and society. She unmasked the worship of the false gods of honour - prestige, power and wealth. She stood against the use of secular force in enforcing religious orthodoxy, she wanted church leaders to be more than administrators and business men but to be people of personal spiritual experience willing and able to listen with empathy to others.

Teresa was not a medieval figure. She was born at the beginning of the modern era sixty-five years after the invention of the moveable type and the widespread distribution of books. She was an enthusiastic reader. Personal reading changed how people saw themselves with a greater sense of the self and interiority. The modern turn to the subject had begun. She was born twenty-three years after the discovery of the New World, the conquest of Granada and the expulsion of the

Jews from Spain. She was two when Luther's 95 theses, was nailed to the church of All Saints in Wittenberg, inaugurating the Protestant Reformation. She was twenty-eight when Copernicus published his ground breaking work on the revolution of the spheres and Vesalius published the first accurate book on human anatomy. You could say this was the beginning of the Scientific Revolution. The Modern era was beginning.

Teresa came from a large and loving family. But one with a skeleton in its cupboard! Her grandfather Juan Sanchez had been condemned at the Inquisition of Toledo in 1485. Her own father, Alonso, had to walk the procession of shame as well. The family were conversos, Jews who had converted to Catholicism. Jewish converts were scapegoats for everything. Racism was the norm.

Teresa's gift to us now is the centrality of Jesus for the Christian life. This came not from her reading or her obedience to church authorities but her own graced experience. She gives us a graphic account in *Life* 8.12-9.4. Her world and her church may have been suspicious of conversos but her God knew her intimately and he accepted her and loved her. This experience changed her life. From being some who sought everyone's approval, who was sickly and even paralysed for three years as a young woman she became a dynamic spiritual mother who listened to the spiritual aspirations of young women, a founder and a writer in the most controversial area of theology in her time - mystical theology or how God's spirit works in human lives. She may well be the patron saint of mid-life transformation.

Teresa writes freely in her works of her faults to encourage those of us who are, like her, not natural religious virtuosi. She tells us she could not meditate due to her lively imagination. The hero of her works is not Teresa but the God who comes to human beings to embrace them and lift them up. We are saved not by our own efforts but God's merciful grace given to us in Jesus.

Teresa's foundational journey from her own need for conversion, not just to appear to be a religious but authentically to be a friend of Christ, to her concern for the broken body of Christ the Church at the Reformation- to pray and work for its healing and unity; and then when hearing of the millions of Indians in America who had not been baptised her heart goes out to all those who have never heard the Gospel of Christ. Her compassion - goes out to all in the world. In Teresa there is no narrowness of vision or spirit. In this she lives that love which is in the heart of God.

Teresa as a founder wanted communities that were open to everyone no matter what their race or class. All were sisters and all were equal. "All must be friends, all must be loved, all must be held dear, all must be helped". There were to be no exclusions. All were to have the freedom to develop their own relationship with Christ through interior prayer. In a world of greed along with honour and shame her first little community of young women in Ávila was a prototype of the future destiny of the world and all creation in Christ. It was an image of the reign of God- that holy communion of all people in peace, and shared exuberant joy. It was a sign in the Church of the dignity of women and the necessary gifts they bring. A sign that the church must be contemplative before it is apostolic. That it must be spiritual, personal and communal before it is ever institutional.

Teresa's vision of the spiritual journey can be understood as a 7 step path of spiritual recovery and discovery which begins with the life-changing conviction that we are deeply loved by God. It is a coming home to oneself from alienation, entering into that beautiful place within ourselves where Christ dwells. Its end is not living in the heavens or cut off from others but living humanly on earth with our feet on the ground praying with our eyes open to see the suffering of our poor, oppressed and excluded brothers and sisters. It means to feel their pain and to work for their relief. It means to want what God wants for us, our churches and our world. It is a contemplation which is remarkably free, loving and alive.

It is a love that does not burn out because it is a love continuously enlivened by the awareness of being loved. We need to learn to lower our protective barriers, to allow ourselves to be loved and to rest in that love so that we may love and work all the more effectively.

Teresa lived this vision in the real world. One that is not that different from ours. She knew the frustrations of incompetent confessors, court cases, unhelpful bishops and superiors. She knew bitter persecution and personal disappointment. It was not a story-tale life of a saint!

Her life was lived in the gritty reality not in dreams. It was a Christian life grounded in the gospels - a life lived with hope and joy in the midst of it all. After she died on 4 October, 1582, at the age of 67 this epigraph was found on a card in her prayer book. Its wisdom can help us day by day:

Let nothing disturb you,
Let nothing dismay you,
All thing pass,
God never changes.

Patience attains all.
Who has God lacks nothing:
God alone suffices.

Greg Burke, OCD

INTRODUCTION

Over a decade ago now, I had a dream. These words were written in my journal. *'Yesterday was the feast of Teresa of Avila. I awoke from a dream in which I had been flying and teaching others the same'*. St Teresa of Avila, a Carmelite nun lived in sixteenth century Spain, yet her wisdom has for long been part of my life, and I am certain, for many others. From early adolescence, these words in a birthday book of sayings profoundly affected me;

> Let nothing afright thee,
> nothing disturb thee,
> All things are passing,
> God never changeth.
> Patience, endurance,
> Attaineth to all
> things.

Those words were never lost on me or forgotten. They remained embedded deep within me over the years, a source of comfort in times of distress. Years later I found that quote and the verse I did not have, and learnt from that final message:

> Who God possesseth
> In nothing is wanting
> Alone God sufficeth

St Teresa of Avila - Found on a bookmark in her breviary.

In this text I endeavor to offer a perspective, based on a conversational approach with a reflection for each mansions to mirror the facets of light found in that wisdom in The Interior Castle written by St Teresa of Avila. Therefore this book does not presume to be a translation, nor any form of psychotherapy or a theological text. A number of translations and biographies exist,to provide you with rich contextual information on Teresa of Avila's life – therefore I do not offer you a biography either, as I am not a biographer.

This book is offered for the beginner – who is ready to set out on their spiritual journey who wishes to know more! The reader is offered in a conversation like way, the every day situation which draws us from God, and then with awareness, back towards God. My intention from the reflections made on 'The Interior Castle', is to reveal facets of wisdom contained within Teresa's text, that illuminate a spiritual pathway for those who seek to set off in pursuit of the holy one, God. It becomes a personal quest for authenticity, of becoming a truly 'whole person', as we draw close to our Creator. By becoming whole we thus evolve as a civilization spiritually, with the desire for peace and goodwill for all. It is about bringing that joy of love incarnate within each of us – to all people who inhabit this earth.

St Teresa's fine expose of The Interior Castle provides a generic model for spiritual growth regardless of what century people have referred to her work, who search for guidelines to understand the soul's journey. Guidelines however, may not always be easily identified as the average person often has to sift through lengthy explanations before a key concept is able to be grasped. Teresa's wisdom is embedded in a 16th Century explanation and formed from her voracious spiritual insights that clearly exhibit noble thoughts of a person who was deeply imbued with a mystical understanding and a passion for God. The difficulty for beginners who would wish to read from the original are the lofty thoughts. Hence The Interior

Castle becomes for many – inaccessible, as it is often difficult to relate to that deep thought, of Teresa of Avila.

The challenge for me! To provide an insightful exploration with reflections on The Interior Castle with colloquial language relevant to the 21st Century, that would encourage a wide reader group who could access that wonderful wisdom of Teresa of Avila.

Simplicity – When the write of this book was discussed with a friend, and that it was to be a spiritual book, it was suggested, 'keep it in simple language'. From that valued opinion, the text has evolved; to simplify the meaning of the pathway for those who are starting out on their soul's journey, and who wish to follow the spiritual understandings of The Interior Castle. Thus it is hoped from a stance of simplicity, a wider readership of St Teresa of Avila will be generated and from that, in this brief new perspective, many will be assisted to have an appreciation of *the great wisdom*, of St Teresa of Avila.

Concepts in adherence to simplicity are therefore formed through colloquial terms, without any lengthy examination on the semiotics of Teresa's thesis, particularly any extrapolation of the descriptive mansions six. Teresa works through her narrative from her valuable insights from the seven mansions as a journey, *a rare spiritual masterpiece* and one that is unable to be ever be reproduced, by even the most discerning person on this earth, as her insights were drawn from her own precious soul experiences. Those insights enable others who follow behind, to catch glimpses of how the soul journeys through the mansions. Your journey too, will present you with your unique insights that emerge from the challenges of the tensions found in your own experience that are a part of the pilgrimage we must all undertake at some stage in our life. The challenge for each person is to search for the questions of life's meaning in our relationship with God.

Exploration becomes the focus for the spiritual search through the mansions to seek the kingdom of heaven within, which Jesus informed us – is near at hand! Reflections provide a new perspective of how each of the seven mansions is important to the soul in the journey. The text has been supplemented with some paraphrased scriptural passages from Matthew's Gospel, [1, 2] and a portion of Psalm 63 provides the source for reflection and an expose for each of the levels of the seven mansions, described by Teresa. This will provide a fresh spiritual insight for fledglings, who have started to fly, and for those would relish a simple approach to understand some of those insights imparted by Teresa of Avila in The Interior Castle.[3] The soul's approach in relationship to God, or as some might prefer to say the Creator, is explained from Teresa's understanding of spiritual growth of the soul. Let us now take a brief look at who Teresa is.

Teresa of Avila

In sixteenth century Spain, other than being a nun in a convent, life for a woman would have been limited to being a wife, a domestic of some kind and the more lurid forms of survival, perhaps to slavery in a brothel! There were few opportunities for any advancement in life, and at that time, a commonality was servitude, an expression that emerges in Teresa's text.

Teresa was born in Avila in 1515 and passed from life in 1582. Teresa became a Carmelite nun in 1535 after entering The Convent of the Incarnation. Her religious life changed in 1555, when Teresa experienced an internal change and turned towards mysticism in her spiritual life. The writing of The Interior Castle evolved from her mystical experiences and inspired by her visions that provide insight, into the soul's journey through the mansions. Teresa of Avila offers us 'hope' in her treatise of The Interior Castle for those who believe that there is a better way to live their life, while we are able to do so. We are offered insight into the kingdom of heaven described by Jesus, as being near at hand, if we have eyes that are able to see it.

In 1455 early printings of the Bible were available, from the first printings of the Gutenberg Bible, of which 2 copies reached Catalan. Perhaps there were more copies available in Teresa's time, some 60 years later. Public access would have been unlikely as copies would have been purchased for either monastic or university use. It is more common that many heard of the teachings from the Old and New Testament, through the oral transmission from sermons. Therefore any personal revelation formed in part from reading the bible, would have been uncommon. To be able to draw illustration to explain the spiritual nature of the soul was indeed a very intimate experience, which Teresa was able to do, even though she may have faced recrimination. There was antipathy by some clerics towards her spiritual revelations.

The soul viewed and described by Teresa from her visions is comprised of many mansions that she saw resembled a crystal castle or diamond. Remember in Teresa's days, that a castle was a normal figure of speech and, in a castle many rooms did exist. The soul journeys through the rooms in each level. The seven mansions represent a progressive stage of spiritual maturity, and can be described as your heaven within, for as in 'heaven there are many mansions'. In the lower mansions, the soul proceeds through a process of cleansing through 'the purgative life' to purification, before the transit is made into the upper mansions. There is the awakening of the soul, then the first illumination, followed by a description of divine union in the last several mansions described by Teresa of Avila. Teresa's intimacy with the divine provides an insight into what is one of indescribable rapture, of a form of spiritual union few will ever experience. But that is not for this readership to think you will achieve a divine union of that kind. Sufficient it may be to practice humbly and with love, the awareness of God within and around you each day, through your transactions with family, friends, work colleagues and others. No matter what their ethnic origin is, or gender and regardless of whether they be from a faith or a non-faith background. Love is inclusive, of all humanity.

Teresa drew attention for that need to journey towards God and the spiritual journey is the ethic, vision and reality of her great work, 'The Interior Castle'. At a time when from the background of a dominant patriarchal model of religion, women were probably not valued much for their spiritual insight and wisdom. However, Teresa's insightfulness led others forward in their soul quests to find God. Her association with John of the Cross encouraged her to speak out and to support her Carmelite sisters in their soul journeying.

For a woman of her time in the 16th Century, which followed close on the heels of the Spanish inquisition, when intense persecutions took place in 1530, Teresa of Avila showed great courage to put her spiritual experiences in writing, at the request of her spiritual director. Over the centuries since, the spiritual insight from her thesis retain their original integrity, and are of value to all. Teresa was later made a Doctor of the Church. Teresa's words have as much importance for people today as then, probably more so now as we have advanced rapidly in industry and technology with the spread of civilisation, yet an emptiness exists in the lives of many who search for answers on life's meaning. People do not want to go deep in order to discover themselves and there is much superficiality in what we participate in, that we call modern day living.

Teresa's embrace of her soul's interior, involved discernment, discipline and her ability to be able to embrace those 'raw parts', of which we all have to work with them. This book offers a way to examine in the first several mansions, the 'raw stuff' that blocks us from growing into a whole person. In those mansions we are given insight into how we must confront our raw 'woundedness'. Where and when do we begin?

The time to commence is whenever we wish to start the long journey into human wholeness. We can't sit forever in retreats to endeavor to have some spiritual insight, to draw out understanding of our own spiritual self. To put it bluntly, we have to live with our self each day. Let me illustrate that more bluntly with this comment made once by a member of the clergy, 'you can visit a McDonald's each day, but you don't become a burger'. Wherever and whenever you start your journey, is indeed a good point – to enable light to penetrate into your soul, to bring insight and for you to become aware!

Soul journeying is not for the fainthearted who would look to forms of consolation that may even be detrimental to their wellbeing. The emphasis is placed onto spiritual growth. It requires for you to be consciously aware of your thought, of how that affects your emotions, your relationships and interactions with others. The spiritual journey is your life task. The journey begins when you have been given the strength to commence that walk with your Creator. God has not created us refined, or perfect, and your responsibility, is to be open to refinement that will enable you to grow. The process of spiritual development enables you to journey forward from where you are able to transcend or overcome obstacles that have been spiritual disabilities in your life that have also impacted on those around you! Therefore the conversation of this text begins with the darkness and rawness of the soul to begin with in the lower mansions. Indeed you may find it raw and confronting, whether you sit at home or are in a retreat!

The reflective insights my book provides, are not intended to become a prescriptive formulae for your soul's growth. Soul growth is to be approached with humility. Teresa provides a model of perfection, embedded in her deep humility that stems from her spiritual desire, for God alone. If we would wish to become perfect we must do so with these words in mind that Jesus said, "… be perfect, therefore, as your heavenly Father is perfect" (Matt 5:48). Everyone must find their own pathway to become perfect without that perfection becoming a form of spiritual hubris for even then, there are snares that lure us into deception.

It is from our insights we then have the ability to step up to, and engage with the journey that will eventually lead us through the process of our own inner transformation. The journey is a pathway towards sanctification, of which becoming *'aware'* is a part of. Briefly, there are four principles of sanctification espoused by Tillich [4] being; increased awareness, increased freedom, increased relatedness and of self transcendence. Tillich said that with an increased awareness, before transcendence there may be found an accompanying sense of guilt and which underlies at a deeper level, feelings of self-rejection, self loathing and disgust, which would all contribute to a low self esteem, and feelings of worthlessness. A negative tension is then often found to be in a person, as they are bound within themselves. It contributes to an antagonism towards others around them, and inflates conflict and tension. One could even argue this hypothesis; that many unresolved issues in life that impinge on the present, might in later years be the cause of illness and distress in a person's life. This would be found to be present in older adults who harbor guilt and suppressed anger, that relate to unresolved issues in life.

Self confrontation is critical – to enable soul growth to be made. Also, the importance assigned to the meaning of the journey, as this journey is one of self discovery. Of what that means for each of us, in our life – in the sense of the eternal self, the other self, the God that is indwelling. Let me now refer back to the confrontation of the self and the 'rawness' that is a part of that. Each evening many are drawn to watch reality shows that are a common part of TV, that look's at the rawness of others!

Quite often, the reality is shocking yet there can also be a humanitarian side to these shows too, as we feel sympathy, hostility, or even admiration for the confrontation of the rawness that challenges us, often out of our complacency. Rawness in every day life is a common factor and we have now come to accept and expect as a part of the exposure to reality TV shows. In Teresa's time, there were no reality shows and her images were drawn from venomous snakes and vipers to provide illustration for the Sisters of the convent, the nature of the rawness of emotion that is able to taint everyday life in those lower mansions.

So, attend to rawness, those ragged emotions – don't mask your pain with camouflage, because God is not deceived! There can be no ambiguity in your explorative journey within, and consider this! Why be outraged at your own rawness, when around you every day you are confronted with the rawness in the lives of others? So when you confront the rawness within, why be horrified by what you see and to wish to be able to portray an image that is more alluring and appealing to others, who indeed might not matter at all, in the greater scheme of your life's journey. The image you thus create for others is the false self. It is not who you really are. And what matters is for you to find out *who you really are*! Attend to the prospect of finding who your true self is, for in the greater scheme of things – *that is all that matters*. It takes courage with a constant slow yielding of our self over to our Creator that gives us that confidence to go forward. We embrace our shadow, and to become friends with it, with all of its rawness and 'woundedness' before healing can begin.

As adults, we must assume a responsibility for our actions that impact on the lives of others around us. To enable healing, wounds that indeed might be still raw require attention through self confrontation. Confrontation of an old hurt that has caused us pain beyond its initial phase of hurt can often last decades, and inhibits spiritual growth. More importantly, it's not healthy. Your body suffers from the hormones released into your system, when you remain aroused and distressed when there is burden placed upon you. Related to the previous comment, is a fact that at a cellular level, *the body remembers*. This was found to be evident in studies undertaken by Arthur Kleinman (1986) [5] who writes of people who experienced post-trauma from the aftermath of the Cultural Revolution in China, who suffered what was known then as, *neurasthenia*. Of course now we recognise the distress of post-traumatic stress disorder and the depression that is a part of that disorder.

Understanding the mind-body's relationship was enhanced through neuroscience in 1993 by Pert (2000). [6] On that subject of describing the physiological and psychological correlation or intracellular molecular biology, Pert concluded there was a biochemical connection that linked the mind and the body. Neuro-peptides form a connective path of an extra-energy level between the mind and physical body that is as yet, not fully understood.

When we experience hurt, the impacts of hormonal release affect the body's physiology. If that baggage of emotional pain is dragged around from week to week, year to year, it will inevitably affect us adversely. Heightened anxiety is an effect experienced from the stress response when hormones are released into the bloodstream. A continual elevation of stress response hormones can over time become affective disorders such as clinical depression that then adversely affects the harmony of the mind/body relationship, where the negative effect of the energy level can impact adversely on a person's spiritual wellbeing.

Therefore it is advisable that attention is paid to attending to one's soul needs. Attending to one's soul can come about in unexpected ways. I watched an episode of the BBC production of the 'Time Team', in which Tony Robinson had in part of his team, a small group of soldiers who suffered from post-traumatic stress from their war experience in Iraq. The soldiers on the archeological dig called themselves, 'Operation Nightingale'.

In that dig that uncovered an old Anglo Saxon site in the UK, skeletons were revealed in long forgotten graves, and from this experience one soldier commented, that he 'had found himself again'. It was perhaps a revelation to him of *the impermanence of life*, that here in front of him lay the remains of people buried over fifteen centuries ago. From that encounter, a part of him may have acknowledged the importance that in the eternal scheme of things, what a small fragment in eternity, our life and death is. Skeletal remains were now the only evidence that a person had ever existed in this life!

When we have issues from the past that impact on our lives now, we need to work with our pain, which becomes a deep corrosive spiritual pain that lies deeply embedded beneath layers of mistrust, guilt, anguish, shame, and to lay it bare so to speak so it does not remain buried deep within us where it can erode our sensibility. We may then become a fragmented, disconsolate person who is bitter and hardened from long ago embattlements with others! This separates us from love, and draws us into a lifetime of negativity. When past issues are dealt with, in an informed and insightful manner, we are able then to journey forward once more into wholeness, of our body, mind and soul. To become all of whom we can become, in this life and to become truly human – to reach our full potential for the sake of others around us and for the growth of our planet Earth.

The soul's passage through the mansions is one where we open ourselves and our hearts in surrender to God's love – and when the light has penetrated our open wounds, there is no other joy to be found, than that of desiring God. Beyond our human comprehension, there is the capacity of our soul, that when laid bare and receptive – desires God only and there is thus a diminished need of other desires in our life. To search for God, we must envisage, entering the castle and making the ascent through the mansions until we reach sight of the summit and it takes time, and our willingness and openness, to search for God.

Begin that journey, with your exploration made through the mansions within the many rooms of your soul, even as raw and confronting as that may be to begin with, as you sift through the silt of painful memories, that have not healed from the past. There is a holy tenderness you will become aware of, when from mansions three on, you become aware of the presence of the divine within you as you move deeper into your mansions.

The movement is from self awareness to a gradual progression towards holiness, and then to become an instrument that reflects the love of God to others throughout our world. We radiate out that light and love to others to illuminate the way for them to also begin the journey to draw closer to God. Please note for many, there may be the need for spiritual support and advice to be sought, it has not been overlooked as it is an important part of your journey for the opportunity to be able to discuss aspects of your journey that are of concern to you and that you also be willing to listen to advice from someone, who has travelled a greater distance than yourself. Journey with truth to throw light into the dark recesses of your soul where God will be revealed as, *'the supreme Truth and that humility is the truth'* (Teresa of Avila, The Interior Castle).

According to the words of Jesus,
"God is spirit and those who worship him, must worship in spirit and truth". (John 4:24 NRSV).

This brief prayer is offered for all who read this book.

O God,
Creator of all life that exist in the universes,
let the living spirit within us,
become our guide to lead us to complete transformation –
to human wholeness,
Amen.

PART ONE

Obstacles to Soul Growth

A writer of Sioux wisdom, Ella Deloria (1944) made a comment in Speaking of Indians, in reference to the American Sioux, *that the concern was, not where the person came from physically, but it was where they were going to, spiritually!* Ella's comment has many implications for our modern society. Why? While we may think we have advanced rapidly materialistically, one might beg the question, what importance is attached to the spirituality of the nations of the world, and of individuals? Teilhard de Chardin, a French Jesuit, philosopher, and paleontologist, spent much time on the excavation of the remains of early humans from long distant pasts. He mused on the early beginnings of humanity, and in 'The Phenomenon of Man', examined the necessary evolvement of human kind, and of what that would mean for human beings. Where are we going too, one might ask, in this Century? The 21st century's rapid evolvement has served to satisfy a hunger for development in areas of industry, technology, commerce, *but* how are our spiritual needs satisfied?

Life is a journey, a search to discover, to reveal so as to understand and derive the meaning attached to many of life's circumstances. But how is the soul ever able to be understood? Indeed some people don't even know who they are in the business of today's world. Our attention is diverted externally where importance is attached to twitter, facebook and ipods etc. It can be very worthwhile when you consider the advent of printing that lifted Europe from darkness into The Renaissance. The same applies to our modern technology, that when used with discretion, can contribute to lift the world spiritually as ideals are shared globally that inspire us. However, one's inner self awareness is impeded when there is unhealthy attachment to technologies, and is counterproductive to soul growth.

Interior silence is deadened when the demands made by modern technology and recurrent events in life, inevitably blocks the silence within, which is replaced by a cacophony – a multitude of sounds that commands attention. Life events take you away from the importance of knowing who you really are! You therefore remain unknown to the most important person. Instead we are inclined to respond to everyone and everything at their beck and call. This constant bombardment creates an internal noise. When interior and external noise compound, it deadens our senses and sensitivity! We need to let go of external distractions that permeate our inner landscape to arbitrate our lives – and instead to take control to develop internal quiet. The practice of silence helps us to engage with our soul, to understand ones self. More discussion on silence is found in mansions five, where the attention is focused on listening within to God, and of becoming still. It is a practice that forms the essential element, to strengthen your ability to communicate interiorly with your soul to engage with the search for the question of the purpose and meaning in your life.

The journey into the interior should become a priority. According to the oracle of Delphi, the signage is to "know oneself". Well to know what, one might ask, what is there to be known? After all, how am 'I' known? Usually it is through our relationships and connection with others: family, children, grandchildren, friends; our environment, the home we occupy that invites others in and nurtures our body, mind and soul; our personal interests and hobbies; our work ethics, whether we are seen as being successful/ unsuccessful, employed/unemployed, retired or whatever! However the 'I' that cares for others, often becomes too busy! By now many of you would have said or heard others say, "I'm too busy". A catch cry that often alienates us from others. But how would it be if we did not attend to the need of our soul – because *we* are too busy! However many are too busy, and perhaps that is symptomatic of the distress of modern society that many experience each and every day.

A question begs to be asked, what else is there in life? Is there something 'I' have missed out on? 'I' am a person who is mindful of others. That 'I' commits to being altruistic – and raises funds and contributes to those not so well off, respects animal welfare, the rights of the marginalised, and so on! How does the 'I' begin that inner journey that Teresa writes of? Indeed, is it even important to do so? The pace of how we have raced throughout life is perhaps the most detrimental obstacle to soul growth fuelled by our own ignorance or lack of awareness, attached to our desires. Desire, forms the basis for our ambition, greed and attachments in life. It is fuelled from a variety of sources around us, based on our own inadequacy. Some might even argue that desire is the stimulant for passion. And passion does drive many, to higher levels of achievement. However, if your desire places an obstacle in the way of your soul growth, it is undesirable!

The race and pace of life When we become entrapped by the surrounds of the material world, it serves to separate us from God. Drawn from racing, several examples are used to illustrate that. In 1 Cor 9:25 the attention is drawn *to what we race for*, will it be to obtain a perishable crown or that which is imperishable? The perishable example is used first. One Tuesday in November, I watched the Melbourne Emirates Cup – a race that almost halts the nation. It seduced me to sit and be entertained to watch great horses combated against each other in that 2 mile race. An Australian horse won. There are always favourites and a 'cheeky' horse *snuck in between* the two favourites, to steal away some of the glamour. Life is like that! Something comes *in between us* and our higher self. It draws us away from our inner self and God. The race lasted a thrilling three minutes and it is now part of history. Each year a Melbourne Cup race will be held with an emergence of new horses, placed for the course, along with owners and trainers who desire to win for their glory a *perishable crown*!

A race of a different kind – inspired the movie 'Chariots of Fire', and was drawn from the life of Eric Liddell, a devout Scottish Christian born in China, whose parents were missionaries there. Eric considered the Olympics his final run before returning to China, to also work as a missionary. Featured in the film, was Harold Abrahams a Jew, who experienced anti-Semitism from the University staff at Cambridge where he worked. Both had previously raced against each other, with Liddell winning the event. In 1924, the races they would each compete in *would be for imperishable crowns*!

In 1924, each man represented Great Britain at the Paris Olympics. Eric decided not to race, as his 100 metres was scheduled on his day of worship. Fortunately, a place on a different day in the 400metres was offered, but it was a much longer race for him. With Eric no longer racing, Harold Abrahams was given a chance to win gold in the 100 metres race. Eric and Harold both raced for their lives, each with a different purpose. Eric ran as he saw to glorify God, and Harold ran a race equally important for humanity, to overcome racial prejudice towards Jews. They each won gold medals for their events. Abrahams returned to the UK to marry his sweetheart Sybil and became a representative for British Athletics. Liddell returned to China to work as a missionary, and later died in his early 40's.

What we race for, is found to be shaped by those values that *govern our desires*. Life can be a race, but it needs to be one that is competitive against your self. Found in 1 Cor 9:24, "Do you not know that at the sports, all the runners run the race, but only one receives the prize? Like them, run to win". Consider your pace and adjust it accordingly to ensure the course is raced smoothly to win the race of your life, to find the divine God within, in the inner sanctum of your soul.

The kingdom of God within

Imagine if those three great virtues of Christian faith referred to as faith, hope and love, were practiced *with righteousness*. The world in which we inhabited would be vastly different. In an interview on ABC1 in November 2013, Yoko Ono discussed her former life with John Lennon. His signature piece, 'Imagine' was briefly aired. Yes, imagine a world that could be a better place, of peace and harmony between Christian, Muslim, Jew, Hindu and Buddhist – all who practiced faithfully with humility and love, the teachings and beliefs of their respective traditions in the pursuit of God, Allah, Krishna and Nirvana.

There would be no further cause for terrorism, weapons of mass destruction, war, rape, murder, torture or exploitation of the earth or its people. The world would be a better place if each person, held the love of God in their heart and inhabited within, the crystal castle of their soul. That castle is yours to inhabit whenever you wish. But work needs to be done by you, before that claim on your castle can be made and a cleansing from the detriment of that which does not sustain you spiritually. In her time on earth, Teresa formed a friendship with St John of the Cross, the author of The Dark Night of the Soul. A brief reference is made to his work, to provide insight on the soul's journey when the soul sets off in pursuit of the beloved. To enter that pursuit, purification through cleansing or sanctification must be made, before any advancement is enabled in one's spiritual growth.

Sanctification is formed around the principles of: an increased awareness, increased freedom, increased relatedness and that of self transcendence that Tillich referred too. Reference is made to 'awareness' here, referred to by Teresa of Avila in her treatise of The Interior Castle. Awareness is found when we first begin to encounter the rooms in the dungeons that form parts of the lower mansion in our internal landscape. As we become aware, we gain insight into what lurks in that internal landscape that impedes our progress towards personal sanctification. From a Buddhist tradition this is recognised as *gaining insight into the self*, through mindful awareness (Nhat Hanh, 2007). [7]

Awareness and insight Let's look briefly at two different traditions that look at awareness and insight. A noted Buddhist nun, leader and an author Pema Chodron [8] said that it was to find out what our true nature is and to speak and act from that. We then become authentic and can advance from that point to become sound in our practice from an increased awareness that will eventually lead to enlightenment. If we lack awareness into our deprived spiritual state, then we lack insight and consequently any progress is unable to be made. Teresa of Avila drew this illustration on the lack of awareness, that whilst ever the soul was held by mortal sin, nothing was ever able to profit it. For even with good works this would not merit towards eternal reward, as the desire of those good works were not intentioned from God as a first principle. Only through God does real virtue proceed, that justifies our virtue. In what they both say, awareness is required for us to grow.

Teresa drew these two inferences; the first is the need for God to be present for the soul in that journey to be made towards sanctification, for without God, the soul is an arid place where fountains of living water are absent, a dry parched land. Second, in such a soul, the inhabitants of the lower mansion described by Teresa, are venomous reptiles and vipers being metaphorically, the emotions, and unpleasant character traits that are negative impediments to our growth. Perhaps those 'venomous reptiles' were a very impressionable way of providing an illustration for the younger sisters of the convents during that time.

Metaphorically, it is on account of the numbers of snakes, vipers and venomous reptiles that inhabit the lower mansions, the soul is prevented from seeing light, it is stuck in this lower realm of tension and anxiety. It writhes there, held by its own relentless tension, where it is not free, but held captive. This inhibits any advancement to the higher mansions, as the person engages with many activities that are more attractive than that of the development of the soul's growth. Teresa's second inference is that without God, the soul cannot proceed in its journey towards sanctification. The soul needs work to be attended to, to be purified and cleansed through God's grace. Your behalf *is a desire to become whole*! Required by you is you forsake all of which drew you into darkness and of selfishness – that separated you from love, and led you away from God.

PART TWO

The awakened soul

A stage in life emerges when the pace of life requires a check made on it, for even the desire for that which was previously perceived as more important and greater in material terms now becomes less. Then the person or rather their soul, seeks sustenance from other sources. Even amidst rainforests, animal rights, human rights and justice, a thirst for a greater knowledge and understanding of life starts to stir within us. This springs from the fountain of life giving essence, and awareness slowly steeps in, as a realisation is made of the beauty of life that surrounds us. According to Teresa, it is the soul that has become 'enlivened' and the connection is then made with God – with the Creator, who is the source of all things, all goodness, virtue and love.

How do we begin to understand the needs of the soul and how we can help our soul to achieve further growth? Simply from the start, there are no easy steps to take and the journey is arduous and long. So be prepared for the next stage of your life, to become a lengthy spiritual sojourn. It is noteworthy to understand that from Teresa of Avila's perspective, the interior castle of the soul is built upon seven levels or mansions, with each level having many rooms. The levels represent a maturation of spiritual understanding that is able to be attained, *by some but not all*, in this earthly life. With the ascent of each progressively higher level, the less likely we are to succeed, as it is both strenuous and arduous, like climbing Mt Everest which few ever do, and requires a lot of preparation and commitment. How much effort we put into that is decided by oneself, as each person has free will. Remember that life is all about preparation when we arrive into incarnation in this world until we finally need to leave and say goodbye. Next the reflections are provided that will assist to provide facets of that journey through the mansions.

The Soul's Journey

Seven reflections are offered for the soul journeyer, to provide insight into each of the mansions of the crystal castle, described by Teresa of Avila. Each brief reflection is made before entering into each mansion with words provided from Psalm 63. There are a number of metaphors used that provide strong impressions on which our thought can be anchored, as our search for God throughout these mansions begins. The words of reflection are expressed by David, and each verse can be repeated often and committed to memory. Spend time with a verse perhaps a week or so on each mansions, to reflect and to go deeply to draw your insight from that well within yourself.

The soul makes the acclamation, 'O God, you are my God', the recognition of the source of its quest. 'Early will I seek you' – signals the intent for David to seek out God as soon as possible! Does he mean earlier on in his life, or perhaps early at the start of each day? David actively attends to seek out God in his life.

O God, You are my God,
Early will I seek you;

A short time ago, in the basement of your mansion the pursuit of your life, was possibly found embedded in that which did not satisfy, which instead led you to a metaphorical desert, where there was no living water to quench your thirst, where after each success, or after each conquest, you felt empty.

In a dry and thirsty land
Where there is no water.

Even when you succeed in the acquisition of all you desired, a thirst remains that cannot be quenched by any consumerable property. That may be why in our madly driven consumer society, where values are forged in the maintenance needs of the physical body, there is found to be a lack of ability, to enliven us and to lift our soul! Temporarily maybe, but after the first flash of joy, a vacuum remains that waits to be filled with more. More of what?

We hear the soul express – it 'thirsts', to be quenched by your love and that the flesh '*longs*' for you, that is to do your will! From this longing to do God's will, you need to develop a pure heart and clean hands. Teresa is attributed to the saying that we are God's hands and feet on this earth, and the soul is as one who would tend to a garden, planting, watering and cultivating. How else would God's work be done on earth? Through you!

My soul thirsts for you;
My flesh longs for you.

The search for God – once begun cannot be delayed as the soul that has longed for God in a '*dry and thirsty land'* set's off on the journey. That is true now just as it was centuries ago, but in a different way. The soul in this century is surrounded by so many distractions, and thirsts for that which can nourish it spiritually. The inner sanctum of the material world, is an illusionary world, and lacks the ability to satisfy the yearning of the soul for very long.

So I have searched for you

So the soul goes on its quest – to search and to find God, '*in the sanctuary*', to look for God in all of the mystery of the 'power and glory' that surrounds that presence. The quest for the luminescent pearl that has evaded you for so long is within reach, and only through God's grace being available to flow through you, to direct you towards it. The fifth mansions are a place where we become impassioned by a deep longing, a thirst and desire for God.

in the sanctuary,

The immense splendour of God is viewed upon the arrival into the sixth mansions, in all of its power and glory. The senses of the soul, the pathways that lead from the external of the castle to the internal are fully cognizant. From this realm, lofty inspirations draw out creation formed from human hands that give glory to God. With eyes fully opened, we see the beauty of that creation, and become co-creators for God, as we engage with a heightened awareness of that need to become part of bringing the vision of a new Eden, into reality.

To see your power and your glory

The reflections lead us step by step, through the different levels of the mansions, to give us further insight, into the spiritual world, that is not derived from adherence to any particular religion, ritual or dogma.

This is the pure realm of soul, and it is yours!
No one else owns this space
Except God.

MANSIONS ONE

Entering the basement

A task in the first mansions:
To understand what we are driven by in life

A place of secrecy is where we hide things away, from ourselves and, as storage area it is usually dark and lacks natural light, an area where some might be a little fearful of entering, for what '*it*' may reveal to us. It is important to note this room being at the bottom of the castle in our first mansions, although it may be on bedrock, might be a shaky foundation on which the home rests upon. How do we know how strong a foundation it is? Does dampness, dry rot and a crumbling mortar, give evidence to that weakness?

As we enter into the basement of our lives, odd assortments of articles can be found. The entanglement of rubbish that resides there is the equivalent of negative emotions that are a part of your life. In order to establish what lies there, and to remove or 'clutter bust', we must not be fearful and make the effort to transport ourselves there to de-clutter each room, and to slowly remove debris, generally to make this place clean, remembering it forms the base on which all else rests.

De-clutter your rubbish in the basement It is important that when you do start to de-clutter your emotional rubbish, you do not dump it onto others. You take the responsibility as it is your rubbish to try to sift through, to make sense of '*it*' and, to do the cleaning out of whatever is there. You don't project it, and blame, or displace it elsewhere. That '*it*' is for you to recognize and to work on, with your soul development. You work on those areas in your life that took precedence over your soul growth, to enable some light to enter into. In a way at this stage, it's a little like walking through darkened rooms, with a torch that has a battery that is old, that flickers on and off. It gives off a very weak light, just enough for you to begin to be able to see your way around. However you will still bump into and stumble over clutter despite the weak light you use to see with.

A place where little or no light penetrates can indeed be a fearful gloomy realm and movies pre-occupied with murder and sadism, are often framed within the context of a basement. Teresa speaks of the basement as if it were a dungeon, where the soul is separated from its Creator. It prefers the darkness of this place, where the internal environment is like a dark stagnant pool. Here the crystal is dull and lacks clarity, and thus is deprived of any opportunity to shine. It remains in this stagnant environment without light.

How does light enter the soul? Teresa says the gate or doorway lies in prayer and meditation. It is not a duty to be performed perfunctorily, but one that should embrace love in the attention to one's inner being and be attended too, often each day. Being a Carmelite required a fierce discipline to be able to arise for prayer in the early hours of each morning. As frail as you now are spiritually, once the soul journey begins, *any effort undertaken with love* – translates into a commitment and diligence. All of the frailties and faults such as; self loathing, guilt, disgust and shame that offer impediments to this journey, need to be driven from the soul. They are to be replaced with love, trust, joy, peace, harmony and a desire to find goodness in one's life. You begin to meditate and the self reflection examines what lies in this cavernous basement. It does not become a morbid pre-occupied self introspection, with a fixation held onto events that occurred years ago. A healthy approach is to *make friends* with those events, with those anxieties and *to let go of them*!

The search begins with that need to understand how you have **'attached'** significant meaning to those past events and of being able to let them go and then to free yourself from that emotional clutter, pain and hurt. This has a greater impact in our later life years, as resentments can build over time that requires on our part, first self forgiveness, and then the forgiveness of others. If we don't heed that need to let go, acrimony – a deep bitterness eats into our soul, and we become a victim rather than a victor, frozen in time, unable to vanquish the past that has prevailed to retain a hold over you, that disempowered you.

An example of letting go is found with respect of the late Nelson Mandela, who overcame spiritual destitution following his long 27 years of incarceration. In 1962, the Africans in a mistaken error of human judgement sentenced a good man whom they accused of sabotage against the government. When he emerged after years of imprisonment at the age of 71 years, he was without bitterness or any desire for revenge. It was evident from his words and actions, that although 'the flower of his life' had been taken away from him in prison – it was important to treat everyone with 'impeccable integrity'. There was no call for vengeance from those who had *misunderstood* him in his desire for the dignity and equality for black and white South Africans. Ironically Mandela's forward movement with life would see him eventually govern as the first black president of South Africa. There is an important conclusion that might be drawn from this for you to consider.

What will help you to move forward with your life? Do you want to remain in a prison that is one of your own creation to remain in this basement of your soul, where *you are never able to see the light, or the glory of God*? Do you want to chip away at rocks each day turning them into fine powder like Nelson did in the prison courtyard? The rocks may well represent all of the negativity you hold in your life. Your release is from that *which you will give to yourself* – forgiveness of yourself and of others. Mandela was a man whose forgiveness was a key factor in his ability to move forward with his life!

No escape from confrontation The soul's interior journey described by Teresa – is not about escape – it is about confrontation! In her wisdom, Pema Chodron pointed out there *was no wisdom* in trying to escape. You are your self – and there is nowhere you can escape from that self. In your soul journey you acknowledge your faults to allow yourself – self forgiveness and the forgiveness of others. This requires a greater effort on your part as it is not easy to examine those negative aspects that create for you – discomfort! Also at this junction, if you have a pre-existing mental illness, or deeply embedded unresolved issues that relate to complicated grief over any life event, a recommendation for you is to *consult with a counselor*. Or, anyone who journey's and feels the need to discuss some of their spiritual insights that confuse them, *might seek the value to have a spiritual adviser*.

Self confrontation is found in the Ignatian *'Examen'*[9], a private conversation that is held between you and God, at the closure of each day, from which self awareness is enhanced. It allows you to filter from your conscience, faults you have identified, and also to have insight into the acquisition of the virtues necessary for you to progress forward. This is a method not all will be comfortable with. Mentioned here it provides us with as an example of 'self confrontation', and of the wisdom of not wishing to escape. After all, wherever you go, do you not take yourself along too? Who would you rather journey through your life with, the self you are now or *who you can become*? Life is about being and becoming. The opportunity is yours, to become a whole person, in mind, body and spirit.

Discipline is required to attend to spiritual growth as you journey. Spiritual discipline is about our commitment, of commitment to a life of interior awareness. Spiritual discipline requires patience and attentiveness. It's not about saying 'mindless' prayer. It is about communing internally and reflectively to offer ourselves to the divine within. You attend to your practice daily – with attentiveness to detail, of what can be garnered from awareness and insight, and the commitment you are prepared to make, that will form and shape who you eventually become in time, as your soul growth enters a spurt and you begin to sense and become aware.

An exodus begins with the journey It is part of our movement in greater faith and deepening spirituality and relationship with God.

A requisition is to sit with clarity, to clutter bust and sift through the muddy silt that impedes the flow of life giving waters to your soul. From a perspective embedded in health care over the past 40 years, I can only suggest that if a person had blocked arteries, would they wish them to be cleared, so that the blood can flow freely to enable life to continue? Where are the living waters that flow to nourish the garden of your soul in this dry and parched land that bares only weeds! How do you wish to start with this irrigation, to bring water to quench the parched soil of your soul?

Transformation will take a long time, it's not about the speed or rapidity of getting a spiritual makeover. Even though you make a start on your clutter busting, inner transformation takes time, unlike the reality shows on TV where we see 24 hour makeovers. Patience and perseverance were stressed as desirable traits to possess, by Teresa. Training to be a super athlete takes years before you can win an Olympic race. That metaphor of training is referred to by the Apostle Paul (1 Cor. 9: 24-27). Training that will become an involvement to grow your soul takes years! Each of the lower mansions and all of the rooms in every mansions takes time for some to be entered, then re-entered, over weeks, months, and years! A lifetime for that soul journey to be made and with almost certainty, few will ever in their lives be able to enter and explore, the upper three mansions, without the divine intervention of God's grace in their lives. And whilst you may find that discomforting, remember Teresa was a saint! You might however consider yourself to be *a saint in progress*. More important it is for you to have the realisation your spiritual growth is an eternal journey!

A final question before we start out on that exploration of the seven mansions. Is the spiritual journey worth the effort? Only you will be able to tell. That will be when you have reached a level of understanding and spiritual insight from your journey in the years ahead from which you are able to look back, to see your progress from whom you once were. Remember, this is about your spiritual wellbeing, just as time and effort is invested into the latest fad diets and exercise regimes to acquire physical wellbeing, the time and effort necessary to cultivate your spiritual wellbeing requires an investment of time and energy and the inspiration to seek that alchemy of the soul, where gold is indeed measured in spiritual terms, not in the physical. Let's look at what you are able to begin to work on, as we reflect on what life is like in the first mansions.

IN THE FIRST MANSIONS
**Reflection–In a dry and thirsty land
Where there is no water. Ps 63**

It is where you endeavor to fill your life,
with everything that can block out the internal silence!
You call it every day living!

This form of living –
is one that puts you on hold, it claims your life,
and does not sometimes allow you time to breathe,
In fact, it can be quite suffocating.
There are so many demands,
that modern day life places upon you.

You prevail in the pursuit
of the constant striving that is a part of this.
You strive for attainment, for success, and yes,
you receive accolades, for all your hard work and effort.
Yet at the end of the day, often it does not sustain you –
to be replaced instead with a feeling of emptiness
and another hurdle steps in front of you,
another race yet to overcome.

There is not much joy –
Yet you continue in the relentless pursuit
of a consumer driven madness.
Day in and day out,
there are events, and circumstances
that drives you – from one event to the other.

The complexity of this form of living,
takes its toll.

Often you may feel of not being in control.
You take time out with short breaks,
whilst your physical body recuperates.

Yet what of your soul care
Who cares for that?
Indeed have you taken time to listen deeply to yourself,
during that time?

Teresa draws attention to – how stupid it would be
for a person not to know their own name!
But what does that person know of their soul,
that dwells intimately within them?
What do they know of their inner nature?

Committing
Teresa said, entering into the castle,
requires attention to the spiritual side of our nature.
This requires discipline often a word we would all rather not hear,
commitment sounds better.
It requires, that prayer or a form of similar devotion is made,
with a commitment to honor God.

That communion with God is beneficial
to the soul, as it attends to in the first instance,
the nurturance of one's internal self.

By prayer a reference is not drawn of those aspects,
such as religious piety and religiosity,
but heartfelt prayer!

Simple heartfelt prayer
can be a silent expression of gratitude,
that rejoices in life, for all that is created.

It is not a shopping list made up of constant requests.
Silent thanks and worship can all be made,
in the temple of our heart,
with the focus on the moment we are in – now.

Time

More than anything time needs to be set aside,
for this event, to sit reflectively, with joy and peace.
It is in fact, giving time and space to yourself.
It is claiming for you, who you are!
How many claim that space or time
I hear you say, when life is so busy, so full!

The question is, what do you *fill it up with*,
that you would happily give up?
To be able to sit alone or be with like minded others
and give over to yourself, some precious time?
It is that simple and yet so conversely difficult.

Does it appeal to you, that you would prefer
to devote all of your time,
to less important things, than to that of your soul, your inner self?

Think carefully.
When do I want to begin to know myself?
Will it be when there has been a catharsis in my life – or
now when I have the opportunity to catch a glimpse,
an insight into whom I am?

Summary – The first mansions is one where *we start to sift through our negative value*s that we have held onto in our lives. De-cluttering your life is the first step forward. It commences the journey from which you will derive your own personal insight, so you can realise your potential to become whole in your mind, body and soul.

Those insights will enable you to move forward with your life. To relinquish that which has been a source of trauma and sorrow from the past, of wounds that have come from many sources and have accumulated *'like a debt'* – over the years. Only one person now remains indebted who has sufficient pride in themselves to inhibit further growth. It is you! You are the only person who can expose the truth to the self.

In the basement 'you' stumble around in the darkness, although you can take a torch to glimpse some of the debris. From the moment of awareness, you sense the enormity of the mess and clutter derived from your own negativity, of character traits that became a source of potential conflict for yourself and others. Teresa refers to *snakes and vipers as being inhabitants of the lower mansions*. Place that in perspective of the twenty first century, where aggression, jealousy, anger, hatred, vindictiveness and worse, revenge for any considered slight or perceived injustice – inhabits your emotional state.

Teresa's metaphorical reference to reptiles portrays the ugly negative raw emotions that each of us carry around each day, ready to lash out onto others, to sink fangs in with venom whenever we feel slighted, humiliated or burdened. Each time though, when you lash out, you only reinforce your own accumulation of emotional debt. Worse – *you unnecessarily wound others*, who also carry their own baggage of debt around, plus what you have dumped upon them. So it goes on, throughout the world, not just in your life, but in everyone's lives.

MANSIONS TWO

Find the pathway for your journey

The task in the second mansions:
The soul thirsts, and sets off in pursuit of God

Now the soul has stirred as if waking from sleep. For the first time it senses that a little light has crept in that has now awakened it. In a way it is a bit like a neglected house that has sat for months, or perhaps even years, without there being any attention paid to any housekeeping to keep it clean and no maintenance kept on it. It remains unloved! And is like living in a darkened house.

The illustration I can best offer you is from when I purchased a deceased estate. Inside the house, every window, even in the toilet and laundry were masked in a heavy laced curtain. From within you could not see out. It was dark! My first task was the removal of the heavy drapes, to let natural light filter in. Rooms were aired as they were musty from a year of being kept locked. One might wonder – *why purchase such a home?* Well the house was sound without any structural defect and it had once been owned by a kindly old gentleman. All it required was love and attention to some minor maintenance, and hard work on the garden! The garden required restoration in the form of irrigation to bring it back to life following its neglect. It required water to stimulate the growth of the fruit trees, that they might fruit again, and to transform the many palms that grew like large weeds everywhere. Overall, it had potential. Just as we all do.

The darkness can be likened to trying to see without clarity. Such a situation can be compared to a person, who puts on the wrong glasses and instead of being able to see with clarity, when they look through the lens there is a heavy opacity or blur that disables them. Imagine how the soul might be that has been contained in a darkened cramp basement? When we see the images of people or children on TV who have been held captive, they hold an expression on their face as if they are frozen, or like an animal caught in the headlights of a car, with their eyes held wide open. Even with 'eyes wide open', there is an emotional reaction to the newness of a situation tinged perhaps by terror. The wide opened eyes lack the capacity to see clearly. The aperture of the lens requires an adjustment to this newly introduced source of light that enters into that area of the brain, from which the retina produces the images that are then able to be seen. A fine tuning of the soul is now required.

Adjustment The stage that follows is a necessary adjustment to this new situation. The eye is described to be the light of the soul by Jesus, who said, "The lamp of the body is the eye. If therefore your eye is good, your whole body will be full of light" (Matt 6:22-23) and elaborated on that to say, that in the situation where the eye is not filled with light, the rest of the body would be in darkness. It is in darkness that we stumble, as if blind to the beauty of the soul that dwells within us. We cling to the walls of our desires and temptations as we stumble around the rooms of this basement, drawn away from the light, and seemingly to remain in the darkness. That is until we start to wake.

Awakening Now that the soul has awakened from the slumber that had as its source negative energy, it has become enlivened! It starts to become aware. Kabir, the Indian mystic and poet of 1440-1518 wrote:

> *O friend awake, and sleep no more! The night is over and gone, would you lose your day also? You have slept for un-numbered ages; this morning will you not awake?*

This verse draws attention for the soul to wake from the sleep that has kept it unconscious.

Becoming awakened is found in the word 'Budh' which means to become *conscious* and is the root of 'Buddhi' which originates from the Sanskrit word, of wisdom, intelligence and vision. Once awake the soul starts to look around for nurturance and nourishment. Tired of being withdrawn in darkness, and now with light that has now begun to filter through, there are new and interesting discoveries to be made in this section of the castle, in the second mansions. Not so much clutter is here, and with more room to move around, one can see a little more clearly to do so. It still remains a place where desire exposes the soul to temptation and thus is able to be drawn back into darkness.

Therefore sustenance is required, something for this newly emerged soul to feed upon. Even now there are many new temptations that emerge such as that which exists in a broad spectrum of spiritual sources for the soul, as it starts on its fledgling way. In the midst of this, the danger to the soul is of being *unaware* of the dangers around it. Teresa says that in this stage, there are many occasions that the soul makes good an escape from those poisonous snakes that can trap it and we should understand that there is a need to avoid them. Thus a need exists to find a pathway that is safe and free from the dangers of the past.

Finding a pathway Many sources of spirituality exist, which like a glutton the soul can feast upon. It is advisable that caution is exercised in this stage of the soul's uplift into light, as many 'different forms of feasting', on the smorgasbord of spiritual food is inadvisable. It can have a debilitating effect on the individual. It is advisable to find one form of spiritual nourishment, and to follow that pathway diligently whatever it is, not deviating to others, but to grow deeply into and to follow that life source of the path, which leads you back to God your Creator. Let's look at how a pathway is defined by two traditions; Buddhism speaks of taking refuge in; the Dharma, in the Sangha, and in the Buddha. Christians would refer to take comfort in; the Gospel of Christ, the Christian community and in the resurrected Christ. A pathway supports a life in which the spiritual journey of the soul can evolve, and in the Christian context involves the world of sacrament and prayer.

With the commencement of the journey, when the soul is overwhelmed by a desire for a longing for truth and spiritual love, it leaves its abode and sets out on a pathway to search for the beloved, the Creator of its soul. Emergence from darkness is made with the transition into the light. Let me briefly refer to St John of the Cross, and his work, The Dark Night of the Soul, [10] a work usually thought by some to be related to some major catharsis in life, even the allusion is drawn by some, that the dark night is the experience of depression! That is not the case.

St John of the Cross refers to, *the purification of the senses*. St John of the Cross began his great venture in the dark night of the soul when he slipped away, with a burning desire to seek out his beloved! Note that a comparison is not made with the Dark Night of the Soul with Teresa of Avila's The Interior Castle.

I refer to The Dark Night, in the sense of *'awakening'* to love, which John described from his spiritual journey. He provides an illuminary on the disabling effect of the loss of senses experienced through the dark night of the soul in the search for God, where a mortification of the senses, from the desires of the flesh ensued. In the dark night of the spirit, the soul struggles once more, this time from the 'withdrawal' of God after having found Him, before there is unification of the senses in the Dark Night of the Spirit with the Divine. This is also described by Teresa, in mansions six and seven of The Interior Castle.

IN THE SECOND MANSIONS
**Reflection – My soul thirsts for you;
My flesh longs for you. Ps. 63**

Many rooms still exist,
though they be filled with a little light,
need to be filled with the development of virtue,
attained from the practice of your recollection and meditation.

Now you have glimpsed a little –
of the sin that lies within, embedded in your selfishness,
and self indulgent ways!
There is the need –
to grow in God's grace and love.

The past with all of its negativity
hatred, self loathing,
arrogance and pride – guilt and distress,
that as 'anxiety' stoked your debility,
in that venom filled life – and of how that disabled you,
requires –
you cast that aside!

Rejoice,
For even if others doubt this possibility – it
is possible for you!
For God has shined light into those dark realms,
and grace has overcome disgrace

This is the effect of grace that is not so much,
grace filled at this stage.
It requires progress to be made as you seek out God,
and to move from the debris,
the obstructions that reduced your life,
to a mere survival.

There is an opportunity to grow
Remember that in this lower mansion,
there will always be temptations,
to be seduced by the charms of the world.
Be on guard if you wish to develop your spiritual self.

It is not important for you to retire away from the world,
be of it but don't apportion priority to remain so attached
to worldly living, you lose yourself into it!
Remember you may still need to earn a living,
and to be part of that world.

Refuge,
Each day, indeed each minute or second of every day,
you can slip away into the sacred space,
that will always bid your welcome.

You don't need to retire into seclusion.
You already have within you,
a place of quiet where you can enjoy time.
To reflect and meditate –
and be with yourself, alone.

Resistance
It is when you start to make progress,
with development of the soul,
that you will come up against resistance.
This is a form of self seduction.

Resistance exists to draw you back, so be aware.
There are or will be others involved,
who will tempt you –
to offer you false hope and agrandisement!
But with eyes that have begun to open –

see with clarity the pitfall that lies before you,
and avoid it!
You will not wish to be with,
that negative association – whatever it may be –
ever in your life again.

These are the fledgling steps of the novice
on his/her journey
into the soul.
Remember it is only you who can enter –
that sacred place.

'Fiat'
Teresa says that this stage of the journey,
is not about our situation that God follows us,
rather it is our doing God's will.

Perseverance is necessary,
to reap the growth of the soul,
that does not succumb to weakness again,
and from these first steps moves on to growth.
The soul leans upon as it were,
on the bosom of God
in whom that soul derives,
much support.
God's spoken word is received by us –
intuitively and through the words of wise people,
spiritual writings, worship and prayer,
even the hardship of illness – can become a signal for growth,
and all assist to throw light, into this new mansion.

Impermanence
A recollection of the dark basement from which you have merged,
reminds you, that all things pass,

that there are illusions in life – we follow unwittingly,
until we are reminded,
of their impermanence.

Teresa says that 'memories' remind us,
of how earthly pleasures fade, as we recall that some,
who have passed away having died suddenly–
are now buried,
beneath the ground and are forgotten.

There is no further peace to be found,
by the soul returning to the basement.
It will offer you no hope for the future,
and would withhold from you, all that is life-giving.

**Remain where you are on the new
pathway to soul growth**

Walk towards this new opportunity to live.
You will then find, if you relinquish yourself, to this journey,
God will direct you –
in ways you never thought possible.

Each day *time* is of the essence,
to set aside,
a quiet time for self reflection and,
to begin that inner life of meditation and prayer.

Find the pathway and stay upon it,
avoiding the temptation to stray –
and be led by delusion and desire
away from the inner self and from God.

Summary Remember Teresa's words, "all things are passing, but God never changeth!" Each Mother's Day, my mother would visit Rookwood cemetery in Sydney, to attend to her mother's grave there and I would accompany her there. Such impressions were for me an early lesson on the impermanence of life. Surrender and acceptance are part of the process of impermanence – that all things are changing! In Pinjarra, Western Australia, there is a gravestone marked for a child, in the churchyard of a small cemetery that overlooks the riverside there. The stone reads, *'Teach me from the heart. Not my will but thine'*! The most important lesson in life we will learn is that of surrender, to God's will! Between the first and second mansions, the soul awakens and desires to do God's will.

There was a need, to clutter bust and remove debris, then began a stage of purification. Consider how purification was attended to in the days when Teresa of Avila walked this earth. For venial sins there would have been penances – of repetitious prayer, self flagellation, and for mortal sin, other penances inflicted. Perhaps different forms of penance exist, our own self flagellation, and memories that burden us psychologically.

We are unable to stop 'whipping' ourselves, caught up in self locution, with an inability to let go. It is self injurious to dwell on negativity. This inhibits us from having a change of heart and instead there is a morbid form of obsessive behavior, with a fixation on the past and becomes a form of self delusion. Often it is unwittingly helped along by others who sabotage any good effort for change we attempt, with hurtful comments like *'a leopard never changes its spots'*! How demeaning our human nature could be compared to a leopard! It dismisses any potential for holiness, *for God's grace to flow into our lives*! Avoid succumbing to what others think of you, as you will be frozen and unable to venture forward. God is love and all forgiving – who encourages your potential to become whole!

PART THREE

Purifying the senses

How can 'Holiness' be approached, when you are soiled and would you even wish too? Unfortunately in our post-modern society, anything goes! However and fortunately, the sacred and the divine are untouchable. For those who wish to enter into the interior castle or the kingdom of heaven, it is only by cleansing oneself and having the attitude or desire that longs to be back in the presence of the ultimate goodness of God, that you might be able to approach that goodness as you begin your pilgrimage.

The 'Camino' in Spain requires that you spend time walking each day, praying and sharing with others, often in primitive conditions, no matter who you are. On the Camino, you are a pilgrim! There is a need to have humility in that undertaking. Pride and arrogance have no place at all. Being a pilgrim allows us to become internal explorers, to examine with careful scrutiny what is required for our spiritual wellbeing, in that internal landscape, which requires work to be attended too, through purification. Purification commences with cleansing.

Purification commences with cleansing. Although in mansions two great emphasis is placed on purifying the senses, it is an ongoing process between the levels of the lower mansions, one to three, where inner cleansing ensues.

Cleansing oneself, refers to the internal not external, as no matter how much one might wash their hands to cleanse them, it is what is on the inside of the self that matters. The defilement that comes from your senses arises in your mind and is what taints you to separate you from the divine and of yourself, from being united in your body, mind and spirit. You may point out that Paul the Apostle who persecuted Christians, had a sudden spontaneous conversion on his road to Damascus. *That does not happen to all of us!*

If you have decided you wish to embark on your soul journey, a humble and clean heart is not one of subservience, but it is one of deep humility and, it will serve you well, all of the days of your life. Then you will not be so easily inclined to fall back into what were the errors of your past. No matter what occurs around you. What are the main senses we need to work on to purify or to eliminate from our inner being? Jesus said in the Beatitudes, 'the pure in heart shall see God!' What prohibits a pure heart? Idolatry and the worship of false idols, the little gods that we have attached importance onto in our lives.

Idolatry is found in the exuberance the lust for life we have in the twenty first century framed within the context of the material world that exists around us and each day is driven by our consumer demands. However, don't blame the media and advertising as it is present everywhere we go. Driving along the road you might be confronted with provocative posts on the back or side of buses, billboards by the roadside, you might even receive ads on your apps and so on. You don't need to take it on board! It is there to draw you into the commercial activity of the world and for you to spend your hard earned money on to satisfy your want for more. *Whatever it is that you desire, that is where you heart is*. You are driven by your own desires: your addictions for sex, for a career, for food, alcohol, indulgent living, workaholic and so on, too much to enumerate here. Your task is to eliminate from your life, that which is idolatry and feeds the source of your own addiction in life. How do we start to move away from that source? The eye of the needle gives you a clue.

Passing through the eye of the needle is perhaps the most difficult concept to grasp as you enter the kingdom of heaven within you. It is the gateway to 'your interior castle' Teresa spoke of. It is up to you, to discover the joy and contentment of that interior castle, the kingdom within, which is very near, but difficult to enter. Entered by the narrow gate, it requires you to have a heart that is humble and undefiled.

The Needles Eye or The Jaffa Gate as it is known is found in the wall surrounding the city of Jerusalem. There a camel had to kneel down to have its burden removed from it back, before it was able to enter the gate. This may be where the saying of Jesus originated from, "It is easier for a camel to go through the eye of a needle than for a rich man to enter the Kingdom of God" (Matt 19:24). Required from you now, is the removal of your heavy load of accumulations you have acquired. A cleansing and removal of that debris – must be undertaken before you are able to approach the holiness, of the inner temple within, and why such emphasis was placed on the rubbish and clutter in the first mansions.

Humility is required, for you to be able to kneel within your heart before the God there and become like the camel at the Jaffa Gate, kneeling to have the removal of its burden taken from its back. You too can likewise remove your load of those burdens, of old habits and ways of thought that have led you from God. *Unburden and lighten up to be able to pass through the Needles Gate.* That unburdening and lightening up requires that the bundles of defilement which every person harbors inside which is hidden from scrutiny, are dropped! Inner cleansing is a necessary part of eliminating desire which caused defilement and found to be linked to that which lies in your heart – what you desire. In Matthew (15:18-20) we see that Jesus addresses defilement like this;

> But what things come out of a mouth has its origins in the heart; and that is what defiles a man. Wicked thoughts, murder, adultery, fornication, theft, perjury, slander – these all proceed from the heart; and these are the things that defile a man.

The point is made with the emphasis attached to the thought. It is *the thought* that produces the action, but by having a thought – has not the act already been seeded within out heart that makes us unclean? Think of that, if you wish to understand desire. In Matthew (23:25-27) we see that Jesus also makes another strong case for cleansing, with this reference for those who parade, as being holy, free from defilement. *He warns* the Pharisees, they are defiled.

> Alas for you, lawyers and Pharisees, hypocrites! You clean the outside of cup and dish which you have filled inside with robbery and self-indulgence. Clean the inside of the cup first; then the outside will be clean also. ... You are like tombs covered with whitewash; they look well from the outside but inside they are full of dead man's bones and all kinds of filth. So it is with you, outside you look like honest men, but inside you are brim-full of hypocrisy and crime.

How terrible it may be, that the basement you have left is uncluttered and you have arrived at the door of the second mansions, still plagued with some defilement. This has a capacity to draw us back to where we were once comfortable, amongst that rubbish! Metaphorically there are a 'whitewashed tombs' around us everywhere that parade an outward display of cleanliness. Corruption exists around us, everywhere and in every institutional setting and the people therein! Open your eyes to see it, to be aware!

Be gentle with yourself opening your eyes slowly so not to become overwhelmed by the sudden transition from the darkness into light, to have the insight to differentiate between that which will help you to progress forward or be harmful. Remember not to feast on everything that appears to be 'spiritual', for there may be many false prophets – that clamour for your attention, in a different way! You will be drawn and tested by that which may well lead you astray. In all organisations there are the wheat and the chaff, dark and the light. Pay attention, see with clarity; don't be drawn, by that which will offer you any short lived consolation. Choose only what will sustain your soul for your pilgrimage.

MANSIONS THREE

Devotion and consolation

**A task in the third mansions:
Obedience to God's will**

When you push your boat out from the shore, like Brendan did with his monks, who braved the Irish and North seas in their exploration – there is no turning back! From thereon, the opportunity for your exploration has begun with your self assurance of the decision to begin this journey, through the mansions of your soul! It involves the deep recognition of that, which will sustain and support you for the years that lie ahead. After all, would you wish that from taking those first faltering steps, to put back on your feet shoes that cramp them and limit your ability to walk forward? I doubt you would. The soul requires good support and nourishment on its journey.

Walking through a supermarket one day, I experienced hunger. Not for all of the processed food that surrounded me, but in the bread department I searched for something that would sustain me. A section was there that had sour dough bread, which I knew agreed with my body, and did not cause any experience of discomfort. After you have entered this mansions of your soul, you will become more discerning, as to what you wish to become involved with and with whom, that nourishes your soul. It requires good solid wholesome life sustaining enactments. Soul sustenance, free of petty nonsense and trivia!

Seek from a deeper well, to quench that thirst. Spiritual writers throughout the centuries from all of the great religious traditions, refer to that which nourishes the soul to become free of any illusion. Illusions in life exist all around us in shopping malls and what we see on our entertainment channels. Illusionary temptations are referred to in Buddhist literature as '*hungry ghosts*', which exist to seduce us back, into the midst of our delusions and thus the illusion becomes a part of our own creation in that basement in the first mansions. There is the need to leave what is dead, behind us! You cannot use rubbish to nourish the newly emerged soul, which seeks nourishment, of a more robust form.

Even your entertainment will seem to lack substance, and discernment will be required for what your eye watches. Programs are available that are able to uplift your spirits. Avoid forms of entertainment that degrade or demean others through any form of sexual exploitation, tasteless humor, aggression and violence. Remember it is about how you nourish your soul! You will no longer experience the need to fill an empty space in your life, with something! New forms of sustenance will be required by you, not that which has become stale and old.

The new cannot mix with the old was pointed out by Jesus who said; "… no one puts a piece of un-shrunk cloth on an old garment; for the patch pulls away from the garment, and the tear is made worse" (Matt 9:16). Once you have begun this journey, your old life that took you away from your inner self, needs to be reviewed by you. It does not mean you run away from your family! It does not mean you leave your job behind! *It means that you are required to transform*! To become a different person – one who is more lovingly compassionate and kind to others, more tolerant and patient, as well as to your self! Think of the difference it will make and of the impact your 'new you' might also have on others around. You may need to revise old habits formed through your acquaintances, and even with your family's expectations and the obligations that are a necessary part of your life.

Recognise the life giving wellsprings that sustain your spiritually and uplift you and conversely that which drains you of your energy! Jesus also made another reference to reinforce the problem of mixing new with old, "Nor do people put new wine into old wineskins, or else the wineskins break, the wine is spilled, and the wineskins are ruined. But they put new wine into new wineskins, and both are preserved" (Matt 9:17). Avoid the old ways which led you into debt, not material debt, but of spiritual impoverishment!

Emptying Let's look briefly at the notion of emptying, as it is an important process of detachment from the old to that which is new.

Kenosis is a term used to describe 'emptying'. The description that I will refer to here is from the verses of the Philippians. Phil 2:5-8.

> Let the same mind be in you that was in Christ Jesus,
> Who though he was in the form of God,
> did not regard *equality* with God
> as something to be exploited,
> but *emptied* himself,
> taking the form of a slave,
> being born in human *likeness*.
> And being found in human form,
> he *humbled* himself
> and became *obedient* to the point of death –
> even death on a cross.

To redact this, one would examine several areas of interest; the same mind, the form of God, equality, emptying, likeness, humbling and obedience. There are perhaps other aspects, but I am going to refer to emptying, obedience and humility.

First *kenosis* or self emptying is that which requires an adjustment to be made, of your opinions, your thoughts and of what you attach value to. How indeed could anyone get over your wall if you have built it up so high, that you are unable to be offered a new life, when you clutch onto your opinions, your beliefs, and refuse to allow any opening for anything new? Everyone has an opinion, but, in our own opinionated way, do we 'listen' to what others have to say, or shut them out? Also, it requires that we relinquish our hold of what was thought, to be previously important.

Let me explain that from a different perspective. There is a story that is told to give people insight into Zen. A professor once visited the monk Nan-in, to inquire about Zen. He was served a cup of tea by Nan-in, who filled the professor's cup and continued to pour until the professor pointed out, 'its overfull, no more will go in'. Nan-in responded that just as the cup was full to overflowing, so too were the thoughts of the professor. [11] How could he benefit from the information offered when he was so full of his own opinion and concern! So too your cup must be emptied, to allow it to be filled with the spirit of God's grace. When your cup is empty, then it can be filled. Self pride, arrogance, the need for approval, all work to vanquish that *kenosis*, and its like pouring tea into an already full cup. Become free of the elements that *keep you full of yourself*!

We become obedient to serving God and as Teresa suggests, the person on the pathway should love God without any self interest attached to that. For those who truly practice humility, seeking a reward for their spiritual practice is unbecoming. The purpose on this pathway is to endure suffering and not to expect consolation. God has not promised any such favour, but has promised life eternal, by those who keep the word of God. Remember that as you journey along, in obedience.

Consider a lesson found in Jesus walking on the water. The narrative is set with Peter as the first to follow Jesus boldly, but his effort to walk with him on the water (Matt 14:22-23) finds Peter sinking. Peter is portrayed as a typical disciple who seeks Jesus and obeys his commands. The obedience consisted in walking on the water, to proceed towards Jesus, who said to him '**Come**'. Peter in the manner of like teacher like student, begins to walk towards Jesus, but then he starts to sink. It is inaccurate to suggest that he walks on the water with Jesus. Rather Peter *begins to walk*, on the water! In discipleship *we begin to walk towards God*. Obedience implies trust, and in his sinking into the water, Jesus catches Peter by the hand and saves him. You too will be given guidance and support as you learn to trust in God.

Humility is also required in this mansion to be able to remain true to the pathway. This requires obedience to the will of God. Teresa stresses humility to be very important and being vigilant to that practice ensures that we are free! It is indeed good, to govern a well regulated house. Teresa suggested that we be vigilant with awareness and alertness, so we may not be the cause of offense to another person, and that we become responsible also, to avoid that occurrence.

One remains on guard, vigilant, so that the basement now cleaned and in good order is kept that way, is safe from being trashed again. Obedience implies that we are diligent with meditation, from which we reflect on to engage with our inner self. We set aside time for that specific purpose and we don't seek out or wish for affirmations in the way of the 'supernatural'. Remember Jesus said, 'it is a wicked and adulterous generation that looked for signs' (Matt 16:1-4).

We let God direct us on this path and we trust and continue to trust, even when we feel our efforts are not being noticed, by God.

IN THE THIRD MANSIONS
Reflection – Early will I seek you Ps. 63

Now that you have attended to the dry rot in your life
that undermined the foundation of your soul –
Can you expect consolation and spiritual visions?
Your hungry appetite for all that is good,
now seeks a reward for my 'goodness'
for all the effort made,
in prayer and meditation.

There is no great reward,
only the consolation found in prayer.
God wants you to be small.
Not in statue, but in a manner,
that is to be gently kind and to grow in love.

This does not mean
you are subservient.
It means you become a servant
to serve all, as Christ did for us!

What greater way to grow,
than to develop compassion,
and love for all around you?
This development of love and compassion,
is greater than that of all the goods,
held in your basement for all those years –
with the fear that restrained your emergence into light.

Those fears
that you would never journey
towards God and find yourself,
are vanquished!

Attachment to fear,
to that loneliness and pain,
have instead been replaced, by virtue.

Gentling the Soul
The bull within has now become gentle.
Before only a glimpse was caught of it –
a whisk of a tail, as it turned and then fled.
To trample and destroy, what had been held onto
in the basement of your soul.
How wonderful it is now, to be able to sit,
to feel the fresh breeze upon your face,
for the first time in years,
released from the prison of that basement
Still, you must remain watchful and be alert.

There it is again!
A sudden surge of anger – a feeling of anxiety.
The pain!

Your guard against falling backwards,
is to remain vigilant.
Now you have caught the bull,
keep hold and discipline this wild beast,
that implores you to tame it!

To become truly human with the potential
to become truly whole,
you must be aware – not to fall backward into wayward ways.

Humility, obedience and emptying,
are the attributes to work upon,
to enable grace to flow in.

Summary I'm going to use an example of when my cat Rosie, caught a baby bird, a tiny 'honey eater', to stress the notion of fledglings used by Teresa to describe the souls advancement. The birds in the area were aware of the cat's presence marked within by her white netted cat run. Somehow this little one got in and was brought by my cat into the living room as a gift for me. Fortunately in the past I have rescued the few that have entered in and they happily flew away – they were adult birds. This one, a baby, was in shock! My attempts to 'get things right' failed and so the fledgling died in the palm of my hand. It was given a resting place deep in the crook of an orange tree, where it was covered with leaves.

The point is – that you are a fledgling and your wings may not be strong enough to endure, long flights into meditation and prayer. Try not to overdo it. You will feel tired and you will wish to succumb to your old ways again. Take each step gently in your new stage of growth, as maturity is a long distance away. Race to claim victory of your self, *but pace yourself* – as you grow with the spiritual pathway you choose to take your refuge in.

Lectio Divina is recommended as an instructive and inductive way to develop an awareness of the divine in our lives, and importantly it will keep you strong in your prayer life for the future. It is also experiential, steeped in the tradition of reading sacred texts. Lectio Divina can be used in private for reflective contemplation. As Lectio can also be used by groups, therefore it may be beneficial to find a community of like minded others, who can provide some form of support for you on the pathway (Lectio Divina - appendix 1.). [12]

Transcending into the higher mansions Transcendence means to overcome a difficulty, after struggling with an obstacle. Often the climb up a mountainside can be quite steep until you reach base, when there is a relief and opportunity to draw breathe and rest before beginning the next climb upwards and beyond. However, as you relax, look to the summit. You will be left in awe of what lies ahead of you. Look back to see the progress made, but always look forward. Be mindful that what lies ahead of you, is sacred ground.

When I journeyed with my thesis write a document of around 100.000 words, Mt Everest featured as my screen saver. Each stage of a completed chapter was dutifully marked with an icon placed on the gradient - until finally one day, the icon was there on the summit! It was an attainment many would have thought impossible, from my disadvantaged working class background from Guildford in Western Sydney. Early childhood schooling left a blemish, when a headmistress reported to my mother, I was a dunce! Perhaps I was then. Her derogatory remark framed for me a lifetime of self doubt. My completed write of the thesis at the age of 64, was a personal challenge to overcome the source of that negativity. Some asked why I needed too. I did not need to I *had to go* up that mountain. Transcending a difficulty is a very important part of our soul's growth. Soul journeying is a lifetime's progress and you are unable to see the progress of your inner journey!

> *Transcendence, leads into an openness,* where there is potential, to be able to do whatever it takes, to overcome any obstacle placed in front of you, and for you to become, truly human, truly alive. Human transcendence is about how your suffering and pain are overcome. This should not be confused or associated with divine transcendence and does not impute that.

> *Transcendence occurs slowly over time.* Think of Mandela, who chipped patiently away at rocks in a prison courtyard for 27 years. Think of others who have overcome themselves to go on to live greater lives that we sometimes hear about. Potential lies in each one of us like a seed ready to give birth

to new life – we need to tend that with our love. Transcendence occurs when love overcomes that which is non life-giving. Grace and love are offered as divine gifts to you.

You are a creation of the divine! The Spirit of God resides within you, as such there is emphasis placed onto 'potentiality'. The potential to become whole, to be in awe of the divine, of the majestic glory of God as it shines before us! That as the peak of Everest marks eternity between heaven and earth, God marks eternity upon your soul, within you. When you realise that you're finally awakened!

Commence a journal. Refer to it often when you self doubt. Celebrate stages of your journey with a ritual. Write down on paper the oppressions of your past that caused pain, from your own making or from others, say a prayer of forgiveness and burn them in a safe place. Allow those embers to ignite 'metaphorically', a sacred fire within you, as the dried clutches of kindling burn steadily *with the love of God in your heart as your true desire as you make the sacred ascent to God to become transformed! It is your journey and your soul!*

Mansions Four

Opening the heart to love

A task in the fourth mansions: is one of surrender

You have entered into a sacred space in this mansions, where you are no longer driven by the lust of life. Instead, you're driven by a deeper longing for love – for the good of all, and to find that goodness, which can then be shared with others. Deep within, a sacred fire has been lit, and now and then, you will catch glimpses of that. It does not rage yet, but there are gentle sparks glowing, the sparks of a desire for the divine, that wait for the last pieces of remaining deadwood to be transmuted, and after which when consumed, will glow as a sacred fire within. It is as if the divine has begun to merge within your inner self. Your quest to roam the rooms of the mansions has commenced in earnest. You have set out on this journey, with that one desire – to search for God.

Don't become intoxicated when you experience that joy within you, remain anchored in the moment, and continue steadily with your spiritual practice, not too much that you lack responsibility for the activities that constitute your ability for every day living. You don't neglect your family! Or spend all day meditating! You have not become a cloistered religious/monk and even if you were, all day is not spent mediating! Pay attention to the need to shoulder your responsibilities each day to attend those activities of daily work, that also can be a vehicle *which drives your desire for God – and for the good and benefit of others in society and the world in which we live.*

Place everything in perspective – set time aside each day that you wish to devote to your interior life and don't forget that you inhabit a physical world! Balance you physical and your spiritual wellbeing with a healthy outlook. There should not be extremes taken as you attend to your new life in your spiritual quest. There should *not be extremes* taken as you attend to your new life in your spiritual quest.

Avoid becoming spiritually proud as that is not becoming of a spiritually awakened person and you would do well, to refer back to the advice given in the third mansions that examined spiritual cleansing. You would not wish to become a white washed tomb, parading your newly found 'spiritual wisdom' to others, as some do!

Humility is the course to follow – to keep the commandment of God's love, secure in your heart. Obedience is of great importance now, and what would it do, if having gained the knowledge of the soul, you squandered that through the 'sin' of *spiritual pride*? In the fourth mansions, the natural world and that of the supernatural are combined, it is where imaginings can have a harmful effect, to manifest and emerge in response to your so called 'spiritual' desires. Harness the energy of creation and understand that what you conceive with your mind – needs to be conceived with 'love' as the chief purpose, not as *some selfish whim or desire that will drive you back down the path*, to a lower mansions!

People dwelling in the fourth mansions, commune with God frequently, through prayer, praise and worship! Engaging in the sacraments, silent communion in a sacred area, reading sacred texts, and to share the vision with like minded others. It will encourage you on this stage of the journey. This brings you in closer contact with divine love. Avoid sharing *this sacred journey* with those who would trivialise you, who from their background lack insight. Many have not even started the journey of the soul, and remain unaware. Remember, humility is the key that enables you to enter into your soul's journey.

The priceless pearl is waiting to be found. Continue this way as you are searching for what Jesus referred too, to his disciples, as a search for a priceless pearl (Matt 13:45-46). The kingdom of heaven, he pointed out, was like a merchant who went out to look for some pearls. Then when he found, a beauty of great value, he went away and sold all that he had, to purchase it! To possess that one pearl, all the others are sold! In those days, there would have been many sacrifices made and lives lost in the Black Sea, when divers went in search of pearls from the giant clams on the sea bed. There was no modern diving gear, and no breathing apparatus. All they had was their ability to hold their breath, as they dove into deep dark water without the aid of technology.

The search for the pearl necessitates that you become a diver into an ancient realm to search for that priceless pearl, as your soul is as old as time eternal. Dive deeply into the realms. You can begin to open the rooms on this mansions floor and start to experience the joy of your emerging spirituality, as new and engaging relationships start to open up with like minded people and with your deepening relationship with God. Before, you were unable to see beyond your own desires, but from your awakened state, you possess insight, into the error of those old habituated ways.

You have commenced that transformative process, only through divine love and God's grace. From here, the view in the fourth mansions and the journey into the higher realms of the castle remains a mystery shrouded in divine love. The preparation that you have undertaken to journey to the fourth mansions, and possibly beyond – requires an intervention as mentioned before. That is, of God's grace to flow unceasingly and it is that grace, which will elevate you into the higher spheres of love, away from the lower mansions.

Spiritual fitness is a term rarely used, as people refer to persistence and attention to prayer throughout the daily life of those who have entered onto the pathway. Again, a reference is made back to the notion of a race from 1 Cor 9:25, "But every athlete goes into strict training" Your fitness is reliant on the effort you put in, and desire for the divine. If we revisit the brief analogy made in the introduction, where did Teresa begin, – we realise that the journey mentioned before, requires much preparation, and is likened to setting out for the ascent of Mount Everest, which few ever manage to achieve.

Those who have not prepared successfully, usually manage to reach the different stages of ascent, of the base levels. Even the greater population of humanity, could not even manage some of those seemingly less strident stages of the ascent. Fitness is paramount, it requires for you to be robust for the ability of your journey ever upward away from the confines of darkness. You do not succumb to half hearted efforts that arise from the temptation to look good in vain ritualistic practices designed to impress others. Your robustness is drawn from a fine tuned inner devotion where you close the door to that room within, with no one else present, except God where you remain in your silent communion.

Diligence and commitment, will make a difference to whether any further stage is attained, in this your soul's journey on this earthly plane. There is a stage marked by holiness, where the transmutation of the soul, is changed from copper to gold, in that purest of alchemies that few will ever know. It is not possible for you to imagine what this is like, and can only be best described from the revelations from Teresa of Avila's writing, of the seventh mansions. It is with a *moderate pace and focus* you will achieve your goal in your spiritual search that holds no bars for those who truly wish to journey to find God.

IN THE FOURTH MANSIONS
Reflection – O God, You are my God. Ps 63

There is struggle yet to be made before that final surrender,
how easy I wish that it could be,
rather than the constant vigilance,
from day to day.
In this mansion my trust – is truly placed,
in you my God!

My internal life of prayer,
is to find that which is sweet and pleasing.
This outweighs the consolation previously sought,
where thought was attached to a need for spiritual consolation.

Now the desire is for a life of internal reflection,
as a part of everyday life.
How good, to 'seek' God within and without –
through prayer, meditation and reflection.

There are two sources of the effect of prayer.
The first is that induced from your own effort.
The second is from the outpouring of God's grace.

Therefore that which is from your own effort,
is limited but not without merit.
Whereas – that which is from God,
flows effortlessly!

Remember many have searched
for the affect,
of spiritual consolation!
The prayer of recollection, is experienced,
by the withdrawal into oneself – through *God's grace*.

Don't be disappointed if you experience naught
as a result of your own effort,
for any pursuit of the pathway is a wonderful step forward,
a victory over a life once squandered in darkness.

The difference when God intervenes,
is the fountain of life continues to steadily flow,
and comes direct to you from the Holy Spirit.
There is an effect upon you,
of an interior softening which produces great joy.
and an outpour of love,
that resembles a gentle fragrance –
of a soft rose perfume.
It is from where the alchemy of the soul,
begins to be consumed –
by the love of God.

The internal lantern has been lit
And once lit – the light is not hidden away.
That internal flame, which now responds to the call –
of the beloved, wishes never to be lost to that –
which it has now found and experiences.

What a splendour it is to behold,
as we gaze into that mansions.
We see for the first time,
this gentle warm glow, an internal fire within the heart,
a warm golden glow of embers now lit.

You become filled with awe and wonder!
At first there is the ardour of the fire,
that must be controlled through mindfulness.
It is not to be regarded as some supernatural phenomena,
to become the subject of idle curiosity,

a speculation for others or yourself!

Only through God's grace,
will this ever be granted to you!
Now you've eased into the rooms of this mansions,
in comparison to the struggle's within –
that was of the lower mansions.

A delightful solace is found within,
in the silence of the interior castle – of the fourth mansions.
This state of recollection,
is the likeness you describe [Teresa]
of a sea urchin or tortoise which withdraws into itself.

By your insight, mindfulness and awareness,
You have found the way forward,
in your search for the divine –
and the mystery behind the door
before you entered into this realm.

Summary In this mansion there are many rooms to be discovered still. Avoid extreme measures in your spiritual practices thinking that you will gain some form of exalted spirituality. That is not what this spiritual quest is at all! You should be aware by now that to continue with soul journeying, the pace in your race has settled down into what might better be described as comfortable, for the first time in a long time, in your life's journey.

You take little notice of others opinions of you, and what they have to say. You remain aware of where you are, with your goal in focus to race towards God. You focus and concentrate and persevere with your life of prayer and meditation. You don't think I can slacken the speed. I'm too busy to set aside time for my morning or evening communion with God. In fact there is a reverse situation where you wish to spend time in silent communion and you must continue with all diligence, to succeed. This is not a race towards God for the sake of someone else! It's about your race with joyfulness towards God, because it's important for you and you desire to win that crown, because you love God.

Remember – Who would you wish to become, given the opportunity in this life on earth? It's not about being a success *for the sake of success*, but for the sake of that love of the divine within. Perseverance and commitment are required, before you even get a glimpse of the loftier heights, found in the higher mansions. Keep the vision of the divine before you, but remember to pace yourself, so as not to fall backwards. Don't rest from God, hunger for that presence, that sense of awe and love, that will bring you everlasting joy. It is your quest for holiness that will be discussed next before venturing further into the higher mansions.

PART FOUR

Your quest for holiness –Tsedeq

Holiness – In the Gospel of Matthew we encounter two explanations for holiness. The first is how the Pharisees were considered to be the legalistic guardians of all that was to do with holiness, armed with ritualistic observances, and in their tithing burdened people and of which John the Baptist was quick to denounce. Jesus pointed out, that unless the righteousness of those who followed him surpassed that of the Pharisees, they would not enter the kingdom of heaven (Matt 5:20). Even still in modern times we see that the legalism of the Pharisees is found in the approach by some religious traditions to religious observance that are formed from Pharisaic values, rather than that formed solely of God.

Second, a focus is made on the observance of a particular practice. A struggle begins – when with our attention we become fixated on an observance, thinking a specific practice may help us to become whole, rather than of the focus of our need to surrender to God's will. This surrender implies we are open to God's grace, and as Therese of the Infant Jesus [13] said following a retreat, 'to become poor', a place where God can come into, that if we were willing to serve as a dwelling for Jesus, we must become so poor it is as if we had nowhere to lay our head! Therese meant we must become poor in spirit, to become empty and choose only, the will of God as our internal guiding compass.

Fiat – The crux of internal guidance is the response to 'fiat' - thy will be done not mine' and is why kenosis or emptying is important, previously described in mansions three. How can God enter, when you are full of yourself? That is the challenge. To seek God in whom we are sanctified and as we do, set out to caste aside all else in the quest to find that peace and joy. Other aspects of life that we attached importance onto are burdens, a bit like the poor camel that had to be unpacked before being able to enter *The Needles Gate at Jerusalem*. There are things we must eventually let go of, as we journey towards God, as we seek the precious pearl. We are enjoined by holiness when we set out on that quest. Holiness is not a task that you are ever able to set as a struggle against self. When it becomes the soul's desire and longing to be united in love with God, the presence of the divine in our ordinary life is sought with love foremost before the thought of any task or struggle! Others who have chosen to seek the divine within, who became mystic's, embraced a spiritual endurance that enabled their soul to witness God's presence in their life. Why then is the notion of struggle made as we enter into the process of sanctification? The word 'struggle' or to struggle with, has been used for a purpose, and is explained next.

The process of sanctification – is not marked by a struggle against others, to become whole, as mentioned earlier where concepts of racing were referred to. Nor by our individual effort to appear impressionable, 'that we are good and holy'. That is sadly a misplaced deception. There is no falsity of an ego driven need here, humility is required. We do not deceive God! *Our struggle is internal.* It's a *holy Jihad* [a holy struggle] within us. When the process that leads to holiness is examined, we find that sanctification does not depend on our performance of certain works and a rigid approach marred by scruples, but is found *in a wholesome desire* to do God's will.

It is that which we would ordinarily do for ourselves, in an extraordinary way, with the love of God as the compass that directs us. From here we are led to a new awareness of how we engage within, in our relationship with God and of that extension of relationship, to others around us. Consider what you may have once done in selfishness that constituted sin through selfishness desire and action that led you away from a sanctifying relationship with God. Instead you are drawn deep into the process of sanctification by the light of the world, away from your interior darkness.

Sanctifying relationship – to determine what a sanctifying relationship is, can be based upon others who have made that internal journey like Teresa of Avila. There are certain characteristics we can glean from her writings which had impact on her life and later, her sanctification. A call to holiness is a call from love, and which we move towards with love, towards the divine. A quote from Thomas a'Kempis, [14] is drawn from to illustrate the notion of sanctification.

> Thus says your beloved, "I am your salvation," your peace and your life. Stay always by my side, and you will find peace. Cast away all the goods of time and seek those of eternity. For what are the passing things but snares for your soul?

The passing 'things' of the world are referred to in Buddhist sacred writing, as illusions. Put in the Judeao-Christian tradition, *it is what we desire* that is described in mansions one! What the heart desires, is where our treasure lies. Or instead the desire becomes the snare that blocks us from progressing towards God – that is unless of course, God is our desire!

The pursuit of holiness leads to sanctity by drawing us close to God to a desire to do all things pleasing for God, and we are filled with that overwhelming longing, deep within our psyche. In modern times there are many things around to snare to the soul that keeps us from engaging in a deeper relationship with God and in communion with others. The mind consumed by worldly affairs, is not focused on eternal life, but only on that which is transient. If we became more aware that our behavior could also assist to transform our lives, and the lives of others, would we choose to act with selfishness or, to love? The invitation to love was extended to us by Jesus, and it is entirely up to us, how we respond. In Matt 20:16, we find "So the last will be first, and the first last. For many are called but few are chosen".

It applies to the issue of the casual laborers in the vineyard who agree to work for the owner, and somehow there arises a question over the distribution of payment for the work done. This is raised by laborers who had worked all day and yet some others who had only worked for a few hours, who were given the same payment for their lesser hours. *The rewards we expect or anticipate that we receive from God, is not ours to question!* A response is found through our willingness to be an active participant, to be led by the divine into sanctification and holiness. First the process of sanctification requires these three considerations:

- Sanctification is a harvest, the fruit of the spirit (Gal. 5:22-23). Our hope of becoming our true selves does not lie in making an effort but in our *response*, in being taken out of our selves.
- Holiness is not a static concept – it is an evolution of our soul.
- When we are sanctified then we are offered like the elements of a sacrament, as a blessing to be given back to nourish others. [15]

Each of those three premises, describe logical steps; we are taken out of ourselves, holiness is a maturational process, of achieving a spiritual maturity through perfection. Holiness is a sacramental grace, it is not ours to achieve, but when received there is an awareness by the recipient that the responsibility attached to this grace, *also implies a concern and responsibility to that of the wellbeing for others.* This may not necessarily be through the action of instrumental good works. Consider how Therese of Lisieux from her cell, prayed for a young man imprisoned before his sentence to death. I am sure that if she had been able too, would willingly have gone to his side to embrace him, instead she spiritually embraced him through her prayer.

It is written In Isaiah 42:6-10, "I, Yahweh, have called you to serve the cause of right: I have taken you by the hand and formed you: I have appointed you as covenant of the people and light of the nations". Saints named and unnamed, from all traditions have become, *exemplars of light within darkness* for all to see. The transformed life is only observable to others who see the effort of our action in living *an authentic transformed life*. It is not from almsgiving or ritualistic practices that were observed in the tradition of the Pharisee. But is embedded in our desire to do what God has commanded, that is to love only from our hearts, and to love our neighbour. This love is not for worldly show and the key is found in the needles eye, through which we enter by the narrow gate only! Like the camel, we kneel before holiness, for that which the soul recognizes as, *'God', you are my God!'* (Ps. 63).

How do we become Holy? 'Tsedeq' Are we 'justified' through a desire to become holy? No. This has the imputation that a desire to be holy is without a need for one to be justified first, before God is involved. *It is God* who pours that grace upon us and through us that we are justified by grace (Titus 3:7). The action of God's grace falling upon us as a tender mercy, renders us cleansed, that makes us 'right' so that we are able to walk on in our spiritual journey.

The need for justification from God is found to be imported from the Hebrew word *'tsedeq'*, of righteousness, justice, right behavior and right standing before God. A false imputation may be made for justification by those who are easily misguided in their own presumptions of being *'self deserving'*. Who feel they should be justified from any wrongful doing of the past – because of their *recent* good works! That is not so! It is God alone who makes us holy and righteous, and God who leads us to sanctity. Not anyone or anything else!

It is a call made by love to respond to that love and it comes when we least expect that call, even in the midst of our own perceived state of unworthiness. This call to love is brought out in the verses of George Herbert who wrote, *"Love bade me welcome; yet my soul drew back"* It recoiled from the invitation not feeling worthy being aware of its sin. "But quick eyed love, observing me … asked if I lacked anything?" A guest I answered worthy to be here. "Love said, 'You shall be he". [16]

This poem in its length discourses on the perception of unworthiness, yet it is that which enables us to be drawn close to God, and then the transformative work of sanctification in us begins. Therefore, you begin to live life anew being cognisant of how you behave now, with a heightened new awareness. In regard to your future life, there is the desire that you need to develop a closer relationship with God! There is hope this will lead to a balanced spiritual practice, and not with any foreground thought that it will make you 'holy'. You will be led on that journey towards the divine in your pilgrimage on this earth, to seek God in the sanctuary of your soul which leads us into mansions five of the soul, and of the transformation that is brought about, by God's grace in your life.

MANSIONS FIVE

The Bridegroom has said 'Come'

The task: – the soul goes off in search of God driven by a passion to find God in the sanctuary

You begin your lofty ascent into the fifth mansions, after what seems an eternity of more intensive work in prayer and meditation. Your soul after it has entered into the sacred place in the fourth mansions, *desired God alone*. For the sake of that love, there is a further ascent where led by love, an inner sanctuary within the fifth mansions is entered. There the soul is held in the tender loving care of the divine. This place is where the soul has longed to be and is *drawn by God alone*. In that place therein vibrates a sacred resonance so strong, a silence that can be overwhelming for those who are not familiar with it. It is like entering a very still forest where not even a drift of wind is heard against leaves or the song of a bird to distract you. There is an echo of silence akin to the Koan, what is the sound of one hand clapping? How can silence be echoed?

Silence is one of the most important elements of soul growth to consider apart from awareness. The silence you enter can absorb you into its centre. It's similar to the lull that occurs between the break of a waves on the beach. The gift of listening was first instilled in me by a Carmelite friend over a decade ago now, who said to me one day as we walked together, 'Pat, listen'. No further conversation was needed as we continued on in silence. In that silence you enter another world, another dimension. Silence is experienced early in the morning before the bustle of households comes to life. It is the time of day when then the stillness echoes the silence.

Silence, "Be still and know that I am God" – listen – how else will you understand your soul? As you slow down in your pace, you will become aware of your own breathe, the rhythm of the in and of the out breath. The desire for the sacred, increases as you journey towards God's sanctuary of love, to where you will be held, lovingly for short periods, perhaps long, for who knows 'what time is' – in the eternal sense, in the prayer of union!

The holding If you can imagine for a moment an innocent child, held lovingly by its mother who gazes upon it with such tender love!

Nestled against the breast of the mother and softly cocooned in the cradle of her arms, where safe and secure no harm can come. An envelopment of love, in the prayer of union, is but the assurance of God's love drawing the soul, deeper into the sanctuary of love, to a love so infinite, that even the soul is unable to comprehend. It is not rapture, but is a loftier state than contemplation, one of adoration, but not marred by any emotional piety!

Indeed the soul is unable to consider emotional attachment to this state of cradling, of loving tenderness. Even if an irrational thought creeps in to consider if this experience were real or a fantasy, it is quickly dismissed by the soul that is now secured in Gods loving care. Teresa says that the soul has reached a level where the vipers are unable to penetrate, but maybe some lazy lizards might try to slip in – a few of those irrational thoughts we have. The deterrent to that is the surety of the soul that draws its strength, solely from God.

God's love secures the soul and the desire for that which is divine. Safely cocooned, the soul is held in a golden glow of loving light that is not able to be adequately described. It encompasses the senses, so that the focus is fixed on that which is divine. Such a state of grace is not achieved from our effort, but is from the summons made by the bridegroom, who beckons you to come, to join him in the banquet hall, *alone*. Few others are invited to attend to join him in this manner, other than those whom the Lord has selected to be privy to have an insight of the fifth mansions. It is not a 'privileged position' that is acquired from any effort! It is a gift from God, who makes this holding of the soul possible, *when you are invited by God*, and by God alone.

Come to the wedding! In Matthew 22:2-3, we are informed that the kingdom of heaven is like a certain king, who sent out by invitation, a request for people to join him at the wedding feast of his son. The servants go out to find those who were invited, and return empty handed, for those who were invited had other things to do *and were too busy!* Remember that back in the first and second mansions, how busy you were that you paid little time to your soul care? It can be likened to your washing being piled up and spilling onto the floor, that even shopping for necessities and other household errands were neglected! It is not pleasant to find yourself, your house in a state of dishevelment. Even more indescribable would be that of neglecting and attending to your soul! But your perseverance and attention to nurturing your inner life has allowed your senses to become focused on your quest, and your search for that which is divine!

The wedding feast allows your senses to be captured as you are enfolded in love, the closest experience of heaven you will have this side of your life. Be found to be worthy and not in contempt of the King when you are invited. In Matt 22:8 the wedding feast was ready, but those who were invited were found not to be worthy. Spiritually prepare yourself and keep to your routine as your all important schedule, to make progress in this stage of your soul growth. For those who think themselves worthy with their own agenda of spiritual hubris, think again. In Matt 22:12 -14 we hear the words of the King, when he entered the wedding hall where there were many guests seated. He addressed a man there who did not have on a wedding garment. "So" he said to him, 'Friend, how did you come in here without a wedding garment? And he was speechless. Then the King said to the servants, 'Bind him hand and foot, take him away and cast him into outer darkness, there will be weeping and gnashing of teeth. "For many are called, but few are chosen."

The emphasis is on the incorrect attire being worn in the presence of the king and this teaching of Jesus finishes with those well know words 'for many are called but few are chosen'. Have you considered why it is that many are called but few are chosen! It's not about forsaking the world, as you can be in it, but not of it. *It is about the effort made towards transformation.* Although God's grace is the transformer, you need to be involved. That is the great Fiat. Imagine if Mary had clung to any notions of her unworthiness, "No I'm sorry Lord, I am not worthy enough, and I need to do …". That is not the way for you to become. You become involved in your transformation, and it is you who makes the effort, to be found worthy. Based on one of the principles of sanctification, *it is your response*, in allowing yourself, to be taken *out of yourself!*

Correct attitude – **a change of heart** - *Metanoia*

Of course this is the effort made in response to the soul's need and to journey with that, until you are invited into the fifth mansions. Correct attitude, means that your desire is aligned to the will of God and with the soul journeying, the movement is inevitably forward into the light, for the purpose of seeking holiness, *for God's sake*. Remember the first mansions were dark where no light penetrated, a place in which no living water flowed, where there was no growth in that stagnant, fetid dank musty old place. Metaphorically – old ideas, wasted emotions, and bigoted attitudes block the potential for spiritual growth. Where is God found in the midst of this? Whilst you have traversed the barriers and transited through the lower mansions, work still remains to be done, a joyful work, which requires vigilance, to not be engaged in any form of self deception. Then *you have* turned around!

Metanoia is a Greek word used to refer to a change, where you turn around. Let's look at this example, it's not theologically tight, but gives a brief illustration of turning away from to a change in direction. You may decide to go into town, and, as you head into town, as you approach the last roundabout, instead of going forward to your destination, you change course, turn and head off in a different direction! You have therefore experienced a turning away from, and towards a new destination. How does this apply to your life? From the insights you have been given from a heightened new awareness, a movement is now required by you to turn from that which led you away from your spiritual life, to where you are able to reconnect and re-engage within.

If you think you are the only one to experience that change, think again, as St Augustine had a change of heart from his early wayward days. His mother, Monica, prayed for him, day and night, that he would turn from ways that had led him off course into a life where selfish desire and lust, led him from God. Monica prayed he would turn around, back to God. Perhaps if we were to be familiar with the humanity of our saints and their errors of the past, it may give courage and incentive to us when we doubt and think that for ourselves, change is impossible! Many great saints have at some stage, *had a change of heart*! A turning as it were away from the old to a new way of life. Sometimes you have to wait centuries to be recognised for your saintliness, so be patient!

What will your change of heart be?

IN THE FIFTH MANSIONS
**Reflection - So I have searched for you
In the sanctuary. Ps 63**

One can only describe this state in the fifth mansions
as the gentleness of that of a loving mother
who has gathered her infant to her breast, to comfort it.
The holding of the infant close to herself,
by the mother –
is a part of the cycle of life.

This holding as it were is likened to,
the cycle led by nature each day.
A state of reverence surpasses awe when –
the sun slips above or below the horizon
and a gentle hush is felt,
that marks the solstice between night and day.

There is a lull –
if you sit and wait patiently for it.
When the hue in the sky changes color,
a golden incandescent glow is shed over the land
as the sun rests for the night or –
rises to summons us to a new day, a new creation.
Then softly and gently, the earth is held
by the sun's orb setting and rising,
as softened rays extend to surround
our earth.

In this mansion,
God holds you lovingly close,
yet there is a slight reluctance on your behalf,
dismissed by you quickly.
You allow that surrender to this holding,

and almost forget to breathe!

The web of gold is woven around you –
and like the spinning of the silkworm, it's cocoon,
is carefully designed to embrace you!

A glimpse of eternity – caught,
and woven into that cocoon's spinning,
wherein God's love has enveloped you.
That glimpse of eternity,
has been viewed much like a double mirror,
that captured the image within an image.

As a reflected image from the source
of true light, from true light.
It can be seen represented by the reflection of light
on a tiny dew drop that rests on a leaf.
It is one that sparkles and captures
the vibrancy of that radiant light.

Your senses are retained,
as you accommodate to the intensity of the moment,
which it seems passes all too quickly.
This state of bliss,
of pure peacefulness

You were led to the window of this mansion,
where light has poured in upon you,
powerfully strong after so long a time,
in the lower mansions.

God has held you gently,
to protect you from yourself.
Your eyes wide open and focused,

have glimpsed the glory of God's creation.
The beauty of creation, your soul!

You desire more of this.
But what you have experienced,
can only ever be encountered through God.
It is not through your doing.
But through God alone!

This wonderful grace, of the prayer of union,
is one that has been prepared,
by your constant devotion of love for God.
It has been given to you by God –
as a gift!

You need now to persist
with you new life of prayer and meditation.
If you only ever experience this *but once*,
it will remain in your memory to refresh your senses.
You – are no longer in a dry and thirsty land
'where there is no water'

Summary The soul is being prepared for God in this holding and it remains like a young child, who is still in need of the mother's nurturance. God has deigned to provide it with grace to sustain it now, after it has endured and persevered in its desire and love for God. Each stage of the journey has been marked by a continual maturation of the soul. The soul has transcended the obstacles that blocked the soul's progress in the lower mansions. You desire no longer to be a part of that former stage of life. An internal state of progress has been made. The crystal has been cleansed by its Creator, and there is what seems to be the substance emerging of diamond clarity that begins to radiate brightness – brilliance! In Buddhist terms this is referred to as the '*diamond awakening*'.

It is the Third Sunday of Advent and along the walkway by the beach of the Silver Sands shoreline I heard the words 'dancing in the wind'. What joy is found in this radiant light! It is as if you dance in the wind for the first time! Free. It was a joyous walk and provided plenty of substance for reflection. Passers by on foot and on bicycle said a hearty 'good morning'! Sometimes in the house of God, this does not always happen with such charity. As Christians, we should bear a more joyous 'witness' for our neighbours, within our communities where we interact with others each day.

Teresa suggests even after our gentle cocooning, maggots in hiding that have not transformed into the caterpillar stage can even invade this stage of our growth. Whilst we have surmounted lizards, vipers and venomous snakes, we must remain vigilant to be free of any form of taint that can chip away at all of the good work attended too. An inflated self esteem, judgments made rashly of others, and even a lack of respect and love for our neighbour, can be symptoms of taint. Pull the wrapping paper away from each person you meet, *and greet the inner spirit of the Christ* that resides therein. If only we understood that.

As I continued my walk along Silver Sands beach Perth, a bob tail lizard slunk along the grassy verge, possibly in search of water in this dry parched land. On the horizon a heat haze hung low over the Indian Ocean. Temperatures would soar for five days between 39 to 41 degrees in one of our hottest heat waves, an expected event in Perth's dry parched summer each year. One might ask, what temperature drives our need to respond to God's call to transform, to seek living water that quench our soul's thirst?

When transformation is desired and we wish to become transformed, we must attend to anything that is an obstacle to that change that prohibits us from the kingdom of heaven within. We do not know when that moment will happen. Our transformation occurs at the moment when the inner sanctum of the soul is met with love and can no longer resist the passage to the beloved. Poets and mystics are perhaps best able to describe this centrifugal action as the soul swirls in delight to dance with the joy to loves call. The awakening is a little of what advent could be for us, for each and every day of our lives, where we are given a glimpse of heaven, right where we are, in the present moment.

Mansions Six

The soul glimpses the splendour of God

Transformation of the soul

The vision of God's power – In the sixth mansions the vision is extended before the soul, of that which lies eternal and separate to that of the world. It is profoundly and majestically a phenomena of joy. It can be likened to the experience of an orchestra whose members play in perfect harmony complemented by choral works, when for instance The Messiah is performed. There is a sense that the work was completed by a sensitive soul. Of his composition, Handel exclaimed, that it were as if the very heavens had opened before him. One perceives this, especially when 'Worthy is the Lamb', is listened to, before the climatic great 'Amen'. The recurrent theme in 'Worthy' is: "… to receive power and riches and wisdom, and strength and honor and glory and blessing" (Rev, 5:12-13). John described from a vision, that thousands of living creatures sang before God, to offer praise and who worshiped the Lamb.

Handel and John had each received a vision of heaven, perhaps based on their own perception of what heaven would be like. What is yours? The same applies to how we perceive God. How do we know what God even looks like when God has never been seen? Even Moses saw a burning bush from which he shielded his eyes when God spoke to him. We can only ever know that God is love, is all powerful and all light.

God is light and love – and in this mansion all of your senses are consumed with love, a love that inflames and impassions you. It's as if, you are intoxicated. Think of a time when you fell in love with someone, for the first time. Your senses were heightened and that is specifically what is happening to you, except it is more intense. To fall in love with God for the first time, light is around you everywhere, reflected in everything. Your senses can be overwhelmed by the experience of seeing the power and glory,

God's presence – will be experienced through spiritual phenomena, even though you may not seek it, it happens! And it is hard to describe to anyone. Now more than ever you need to be careful in whom you confide who is trustworthy with a spiritual understanding. *Find a skilled spiritual director who is able to discuss this with you.*

Be careful with whom you 'open up to' as some people, may even set you back through their doubt and disbelief. Even Teresa had a problem when confiding her spiritual experiences to one priest, one who had not understood her. Later, St John of the Cross assisted her with her spiritual confessions. That is why in the first mansions, it is cautioned for someone who has any underlying mental illness, to seek out a counselor before embarking on the journey of the soul. There runs a very fine line *between genuine mysticism* and those who have a diagnosed mental illness.

For one moment let us look briefly at Francis of Assisi, who had fallen in love with God. And who to the consternation of his wealthy merchant father – threw expensive bales of cloth to the poor of Assisi. Consider that in our modern society, a person who has had an intense spiritual experience may be diagnosed, and then even labeled as being psychotic. How many have unfortunately ended their days in former times, with misdiagnosis by medical practitioners who were not able to understand at a spiritual level what was happening to the patient! Fortunately now, with the advent of clinical pastoral care, that has changed.

The point being made is that modern medicine separated the psyche from the somatic, thanks to Descartian dualistic thought. 'I think therefore I am'. One day, with further advances in medicine there will be a fully functional form of wholistic care that acknowledges the interconnection between the mind, body and soul. It is spoken of now with more respect – but in token terms and is not an adequate form of humanistic medicine that offers a holistic approach. Especially now when many experience post traumatic stress disorders and depression, a fatigue of the soul, that requires attention to their spiritual life.

When the senses are assailed or bombarded with negativity, it shuts down the ability of the soul to grow. Instead those people become deadened by over stimuli, a little like over watering a plant that weakens the plant and even destroys it. Therefore there is a need to be aware that the soul has experienced an assault of it's 'senses' – can be said to be spiritually ill and fatigued!

The senses are companions of the soul – that stimulate and delight, through that which is seen, heard, touched, tasted and smelt. Obviously the senses are there for the purpose of both the positive and negative values that are held in our lives. When John of the Cross, experienced the Dark Night of the Senses, his senses were temporarily withdrawn from him, as he experienced a separation from God – after he had found God.

In the sixth mansions, the senses are suspended by God, yet are present in participation of the awe experienced as the soul observes the power and glory of the divine. There is a feeling of great joy and love, as the soul fully awakened, responds to the call of love that opened the heart, and Teresa referred to this as being, 'the dilation of the heart'. The heart now softened experiences joy and a deeper sense of peace than ever before.

A sense of that call to love is experienced by all of humankind, awakening to the power of God's love, of the divine indwelling one. It is evident in our lives and surrounds us, from those who have become transformed even though it may not be seen by us, and who are ambassadors of light for the world regardless of what affiliation or background they are from. Nelson Mandela, Martin Luther King, Dorothy Day, Rosa Parkes, Mary MacKillop, Edith Stein, Simone Weil, Malala Yousafzai. There are many who have advanced forward.

The power of God's love – is evident in our tangible world. An event occurred during The First World War when the opposing troops, German and English stopped at midnight, to sing carols. Truly this was a manifestation of divine power and love – sadly even though they would go on to pick up their weapons of war once more, to fight for their respective countries. The point of this discussion is that God's power and splendour has the capacity to change people's hearts and their lives.

Transforming moments – Once, I sat by the bedside of an elderly nun in the late stages of her illness, which she died from several days after. From a trance like state, and with a look of joy on her face, Sister exclaimed, *"It's just like a beautiful garden, a beautiful garden"*. Was she hallucinating? I think not, as directly afterwards, she was able to communicate with the nurse who came into her room to take her blood pressure. When she made her exclamation, she was transformed as she stared straight ahead. At who or what! An elderly man, once a lawyer in his younger days, whom I also attended too, had a strong spiritual experience. Two carers rushed to get me from my tea break to witness this event. We three stood there and gaped as this man sat bolt upright, and repeatedly said, *"The power of God is definitely love"*, until whatever vision he had, faded. His face was lit up, a joy to see, transformed from the stubborn harsh face we viewed each day.

In their final approach to death, each person was temporarily transformed. Spiritual insights such as these, point the way to a different world. Had they glimpsed a hint of the glory and power of God? Acceptance of a spiritual experience is also an issue here. It is important to recognize that a person's deeply revealed spiritual experience is not written off, as some imagined phenomena, which can often happen, especially with the elderly.

Soul transformation – Transformation is the final stage of being free completely from the past, of allowing that which is dead to die! When Jesus made his radical call to discipleship, he said 'Let the dead bury the dead'. Literally, can this be interpreted that the past is dead? For those who wish to follow God, there is no room for competition from those things, our previous desires that held us. The new demand is to walk free and away from the past, from the restraint it held, that blocked you from journeying down the path – to where you are now. Into God's hands, to be transformed into a whole person! God's love is a transforming power. When the capacity for transformation has occurred, we are in communion with the revelation of that glory.

The power of God is love! Once the fire of love burns deeply in your soul, there is no time to consider the arbitrary aspects of life. When you have become enlightened, and light is the predominant source of the spiritual life force within you, an opportunity exists for you to look at the bigger picture of life, and where God is to be found there. There are plenty of opportunities around from where you can become involved to bring about change. Where darkness and light cohabit, assist others *to overcome fear* with love from where they have been crippled by an inability to let go of the past. Now, to bring light into their lives too!

The light that illumines us is that which comes of light from light (John 1:9). We become *a part of* that power and glory *when we become co-creators in this life* and are part of the magnificence of the mustard tree that once sprang from a tiny seed. Plant the seed now in your life, water it and enable it to flourish by waters that are drawn from the living water that flows to you from the grace of God.

IN THE SIXTH MANSIONS
Reflection – To see your power and your glory Ps. 63

Now may we find true joy as God hold's us in eternal time
secured through love incarnate and
revealed to us
as Christ, the light of the world.

The joy found within,
is stoked by a flame
ignited by a sacred fire.

This causes the soul to be transmuted by love.

This transmutation as it were,
has changed the reflections deep within the soul
to bring light in.

Light
first filtered in, then slowly poured in,
to fill the soul with light
sent by God's grace!
Now light shines ever more brightly within.

Yet visually we fail to see it.
Others may perceive a glow
that comes forth from a person!

That glow comes from the inner soul
that permeates the internal and the external,
to give light to all around!

We become light bearers to the world
God's hands and feet –
in this world.

That is how God works through us,
to bring about transformation to this world
as light bearers from all four corners of the world,
who work together yet unknowingly of each other
who form this network that spans the globe
of this our planet earth.

"Once that lamp has been lit
It should not be hidden under a basket
But placed on a lampstand,
And it gives light to all who are in the house.

Let your light shine
Before men,
That they may seek your good works
And glorify
Your Father in heaven".
Matt 5:15-16

We see the power and the glory
in all that surrounds us
In the light –
from the light –
and through the light
'Lumen de lumine'

Summary Lumen de lumine - *'light from light'* is found in the profession of faith used in Christian liturgy. God from God, Light from Light True God from true God. This is light that is able to find its way into the darkest of dwelling places and of course includes the darkness that can obscure the growth of the soul. Within each of us light coexists with darkness and girds the very fabric of this world we inhabit. It is customary for different cultures and religious traditions to celebrate the light. The Jewish festival of Hanukkah is held each year, and the candles of the Menorah, a seven branched candelabrum, are lit for each of the eight days of the annual event with the final being lit on the last night. The festival signifies the rededication of the Holy Temple of Jerusalem.

Each year Christians pay homage to the light that came into this world, as God incarnate in Jesus with nativity scenes in churches throughout the world. Usually a nice sanitised version of that event is forever presented. Clean hay, peaceful creatures looking lovingly at the babe and a mother who adores him. Consider the reality; a dirty manger, bellowing animals, stained straw on the floor, perhaps even animal droppings, and there standing by the anxious first time mother, an equally anxious spouse, Joseph. In the midst of chaos, this incarnation of light is created, in that humble manger, filled with God's creation, of human *and* of animal kind. All drawn together in a fragile setting, held by light that has made a humble area, into one that is sacred! Modern day chaos now spoils how we often prepare in that lead up to Christmas as we rush – in our business to get things ready.

We behave like children, when we want the 'spoils of Christmas' and not the light that radiates from within the manger. It is *in* the recognition of the incarnation, that we are re-birthed too. *We share in that incarnation through the embodiment of God's love.* This is a final stage in our own journey to our own Bethlehem. Then we truly start the sacred walk to become a spiritual being inhabited within a physical body. We desire relationship and that experience of God, to witness that power and glory in our life.

Epiphany – It is the day after Christmas, and along with several others I have been invited to celebrate the season with a friend, whom I met ten years ago at Murdoch University Perth, when we both studied theology there. Clara described an experience to us of when she recently observed a star in the early morning sky and the impact it had on her and the thought that came through, to slow down. *It sounded like an epiphany.* Clara went on to tell us how she had visited her daughter in law down the road shortly after this event, and a man who lived next door and whom she had never spoken too before, disclosed he had cancer and not long to live. She described how she took his hand to hold it. God worked through her at that point in time to be a comfort for that man.

It happened that on that day, I had with me an early draft of this chapter. Away from the earshot of the others, I followed her out to the kitchen, and read some of the content to her. "But that describes what I had experienced!" she said. It surprised both of us, and cannot be dismissed as 'serendipity'! This is when the mind conjures up an excuse, to produce a 'false prophet' in the midst of that, which has come as a gift from God.

How rationale and right brained we have become, and divorced from the spiritual and creative! This causes us to be separate from whom we really are. People of light! People of God! The truly unified mind is both creative and rational with the capacity that enables us to engage with our creative energy and of our spirituality in the quest for our human wholeness!

Caution is required for Mansions Six

The Diagnostic and Statistical Manual of Mental Disorders DSM-1 first published in 1952 [current DSM-V] of the American Psychiatric Association, [17] provides modern day insight into the classification of *specific conditions that define mental illness*. It is not wise to provide extrapolated interpretation on what Teresa explained from the stance of 16th century thought and of her experience as a genuine mystic. It is certainly not desirable for anyone to seek out ecstatic trance like states. Locution is briefly outlined here. Teresa pointed out that words addressed to the soul can come from; the imagination, evil, and of course, from the imaginings of those who might think God speaks to them.

Teresa speaks of well intentioned people with *vivid imaginations* who surmise they have heard God speaking to them. This form of locution is not a direct message from God and is distorted and fanciful and as Teresa said is likely found in those who are anxious, or depressed. Another form of imagined communication is one that often leaves the person in a state of agitation and extreme anxiety. Jumbled words that are quickly forgotten, might have offered destructive advice to harm others, as well as themselves. These symptoms are found in those who suffer *delusion or other forms of mental illness.*

Teresa also said, that communication that comes from God with origin in either the inferior or superior part of the soul, *is clear and coherent.* The person receives reassurance that all will be well, and gives the person a great peace and calm. Another sign that the communication is from God, is that the memory remembers the words spoken and as brief as they may be, they are never forgotten, but remain embedded in the soul and the psyche. The soul is left in a state of reverence that brims with love, with the desire to be consecrated to the service of God whilst alive on this earth.

MANSIONS SEVEN

The soul willingly follows God to the ends of this earth

As a new creation:
Endurance is for love's sake alone –
for the soul is wed by a divine union to God

In the seventh mansions light radiates and permeates – to the furthest corner of the soul. Even in the midst of this, the soul might also encounter anguish, suffering much pain, as a trial sent by God. Always *when there is a need for transformation*, a trial of pain and suffering is sent for the transformation to be completed. It is as Teresa writes '*Can ye drink the chalice that I shall drink?*' This is the invitation to be wounded, to suffer and endure for the sake of love, for that which is divine. How many are prepared to do that? A theodicy of suffering has been with humankind throughout the centuries, and will remain until the end of time.

Suffering – is epitomized in the Book of Job, where poor Job loses everything, his wife, his family, his cattle, his home, and then is informed by his 'wise' friends that he, Job, is to blame for all of that! How must Job have felt, when even his friends did not believe in him. Job then challenged God, for why his suffering had happened. God instead asks Job, where was Job, when He created the universe? That is the mystery. Some point to the fact as Job's friends did, that we suffer because we deserve to suffer for some wrongdoing! Jesus disputed that way of thought (Luke 13:1-5). Following his destitution, Job had his life and dignity restored back to him by God.

Suffering and pain, can either ennoble the soul or cause it to become bitter and twisted. Full of unforgiveness, a lack of empathy exists and the soul is left to atrophy. The full extent of suffering is found in our endurance, and of how we would wish to imitate Christ, to take up our cross and bear what is ours to experience. Teresa spoke of darts of love that pierced the heart, to cause a sacred pain. Rather than to desire what Teresa experienced, we might consider this, how can there be *depth* in love and compassion, when a person has never experienced any pain and anguish? It is a part of our transformation, into what we always knew we could become. Christ like! Our suffering weds us to Christ, in a preparation for that final union of the divine.

Spiritual union In this mansion there is the union of spirit and soul with the divine, which is all encompassing and all consuming. A rapture of the spirit ensues during which it is revealed to the senses, as if by intellectual vision. This vision reveals that now there is an indwelling of the Holy Trinity, who are present in the soul and, who will continue to abide therein. With this great joy, there is the realisation to the soul, of that indwelling of the Holy Trinity.

On the strength of this, the soul is ready to lay down its life, for God or indeed to go to the very ends of the earth, in the loving service for all of God's people. More than ever, there is the great need for civilisation to advance morally *and* spiritually as we witness the corruption and the terrible evil in humanity throughout the world. From the experience of this communion with God, the soul would wish to become heroic in any capacity to fulfill God's will on earth and to contribute towards the evolution of humanity in that great journey, towards union with God.

Through the grace of God you have become holy even though you do not know it, other than to be impassioned with a desire to serve God. Our state of holiness as a sacramental grace, it is not ours to achieve independently, through any effort made by us at all. It is the work of God and of the Holy Spirit. When the process of sanctification is received, there is the awareness by the recipient that a responsibility is attached to this grace for the concern for others. Discuss this with a competent spiritual adviser and no-one else, for there are still many 'doubting Thomas' around who would try to ridicule you and that may cause distress.

However the soul has reached a stage of growth, where at the inner core, is at peace, and whatever happens around, it remains in a state of equilibrium. Be ever vigilant though. Remember that with advancement through the mansions, many are walking around in the basement as you did previously, and lack insight and awareness. Guard your precious pearl now. Do not caste pearls before swine otherwise they might trample over it. Remain humble, treasure God's precious sacred gift.

Teresa of Avila drew that the stages of soul growth are similar to that found in metamorphosis; the caterpillar, chrysalis, and finally the emergence of a beautiful butterfly to illustrate to her Sisters, that transformation is a process of gradual change. As the soul grows, transformation is supported by grace and through the continual nourishment by the sacraments, and by abiding within that sacred space where God is found at the core. And there at the core with transformation complete, the soul rejoices, and proclaims accordingly, the love of God as the soul's central desire and refuge. This is illustrated in some of that final verse of David's Psalm, 63;

> My soul is satisfied as with a rich feast,
> my mouth praises you with joyful lips.
>
> My soul clings to you;
> Your right had holds me fast

When transformation has taken place, that illumination enables wisdom to be a part of your daily encounters, but always remain humble and have gratitude in your heart, being ever ready to respond to God's will. Our life is about seeking to carry out the will of God and not your own will where in the early stages of life it was frittered away on trivia – and on empty clay vessels. Your heart is now enfolded in grace and love. With your new heart of loving compassion, extend that *towards all humankind*, for each person who walks on earth, is a creation of God. Yet many still remain in darkness, while others have become illumined!

Transformation through change in your attitude and what you desire occurs at different times throughout the mansions, it is a process that is gradual, however in the seventh mansions you are wholly transformed as a *'new creation'* in Christ. That transformation is now complete. Interestingly several decades ago, a toy known as the transformer was popular amongst children who held a fascination for it, as it had many different parts that could be added to change the nature of the toy. A pity that many adults remain preoccupied with their outer transformation, and consider it unimportant to attend to their inner transformation. Instead many cling to what is comfortable and secure in their lower mansions. Many store for themselves, earthly treasures and continue to fall backwards, into idolatry for that which is perishable.

If anyone has ever seen the Chinese collection of the Terracotta Army of Warriors and Horses, a funeral accompaniment of the first emperor of China [210-209 BC], you will realise the importance of the perishable. One would wonder what thought was behind a tomb to be guarded by such a vast quantity of clay sculpted into 8.000 warriors, chariots, and many horses. From whom would they guard against? There was no safety in their vast numbers, as how utterly entrenched in an underground mausoleum they were! Little hope for them there, other than that of death and decay.

What a vast difference there is in the world of God, which is of spirit and life eternal, compared to the temporal, which is passing! Thus our earthen vessels become a receptacle in which God's grace is poured into and received, "Therefore we do not lose heart, for if our outer person is decaying, our inner person is being renewed day by day" (2 Corinthians, 4:16). Transformation is explained well by the Apostle Paul (2 Corinthians, 5:17) "If anyone is united in Christ, 'they are a new creation'; the old order has gone and the new begun". In the lower mansions, obstacles to the soul's journey were necessarily encountered and needed to be transcended even though at times, the obstacles seemed to be insurmountable. But reconciliation to God was made possible through Jesus Christ.

When divine union is encountered in mansions seven, the new creation that Paul speaks of, *is not a cerebral condition*, but is a completion, where you become Christ like. You no longer cling to any part of that which was the old way of life, you have to let go, in order that you could become all that God wanted you to become, from the moment when you were first created and knitted together in your mother's womb (Ps. 139). From those fragile moments until you were born into the world and grew, through all of life's stages, until you have slowly made that journey back to God, as any pilgrim does in their search for God.

IN THE SEVENTH MANSIONS
**Reflection – My soul follows close behind you;
Your right hand upholds me. Ps 63**

In this mansion experience the
full intensity of God's love.
Words are inadequate to describe.

You are rendered powerless,
By a radiant light that surrounds you,
a golden shimmering light that glows
That envelops you in a transforming moment of union.

In this state, the senses are withdraw completely
into timelessness –
You remain unaware of minutes or longer,
in this divine state of love.
as a sensation of pain sears the heart,
Almost as if you experience –
an attack of the heart.

That is until you fall silent, and surrender
To allow yourself – to be
engulfed by God's presence
and to merge into that radiance of light
as it floods your whole being
with love
and your senses are withdrawn.

The pain within the chamber of your heart
can only be best describe as a sacred pain
in the private depth of the souls inner chamber.
It's very core!
Where the Bridegroom has commanded you!

When later your senses re-engage with your surroundings,
there is an unspeakable sense of joy,
of that experience –

Now
Trust in God alone
for God sufficeth in all matters
Of the soul!

The incredible joy, is one you would desire
to experience again.
But it may never happen to you again
in your lifetime on earth.
The greatest gift of love!
The soul flooded by divine Light,
has an irradiant glow within,
like a slowly burning lantern.

Hereafter from that time when you entered –
that holy of holies,
of the inner sanctuary,
life will never be the same for you.
You will be impassioned,
for the state of the people of the world,
and their becoming.

Throughout your life you will be held
in awe and by profound reverence,
of that one sacred moment of great joy.

It is all you will need
to convince you of the everlasting life
that will become yours – in eternity.
It has been a revelation to you

of the love of God that is incomprehensible,
all powerful, all majestic.

Finis.

Alone God Sufficeth - for our Transformation

As the divine engaged within, to unite soul and spirit, the full potential to become a spiritual being, within an earthly body has been realised. You became consecrated to God through that divine union and, are now willing to lay aside your own life for the greater good and the capacity to serve others. You are an heir of the kingdom of God upon earth, and become a representative for Christ on earth. As a representative of Christ, you are now a vehicle driven by love – the hands and feet for God, to co-create and to assist God, to build up the kingdom of love. It is only through human compassion, kindness and love, we become worthwhile heirs' to the kingdom of heaven within each and every soul, willing to respond to the call of love.

As a young child of around the age of ten, I can remember standing at the Jamieson Valley Lookout in the Blue Mountains of Sydney NSW. My memory is very clear of when I stood there and wondered if all the people of the world could ever fit into that space of Jamieson Valley! Now I wonder how all of the world's people can become full of the Spirit of God to transform and fill them with love instead of the negativity that is a part of our planet. Such a concept can only be understood when it is recognised that spirit and matter are both very different forms of energy.

Griffiths, in the 'Return to the Centre' [18] explained that notion well when he wrote, "It is like measuring the ocean. We are plunged in the ocean, we are immersed in it, the drop of water is dissolved in it, but we still cannot comprehend it". That in itself gives us the final insight into how the splendour and greatness of God can never be comprehended by a human mind, and of how the seemingly impossible becomes possible. We might try, to understand God's greatness, but there is a limit to our capacity to be able to say with certitude, 'that's it!' *Faith however, takes over*, while we wait eagerly for God to respond to us, to invite us to that wedding feast. Let us go willingly and with great joy in our hearts to that feast, whenever we are invited.

'Breath on me, breathe of God', a hymn composed by Charles Lockhart in 1791, has words, within the verse, that signals our readiness for growth into holiness, "… until the earthly part of me glows with the fire divine". Earthly parts correspond to our desires, governed by our will, and not God's. This hymn illustrates that essential transformative element, for without which, transformation is impossible, where God's spirit pours into our human frailty, to ignite the divine fire of the soul within *your Crystal Palace.*

Once that light has lightened us, we reflect that divine light that extends to us from God to others. That light radiates joy and love so others too might be inspired to begin the walk on their pathway towards transformation. But following your ascent up the mountain, you cannot remain there, as you would become separate from others, who need your insight and wisdom, because with the new person in Christ, comes a responsibility!

There is another journey required of you now you have completed this journey. You can choose to retire through disengagement or you can re-integrate into the market place, into that part of the 'ordinariness of life' to bring your self there with your newly awakened wisdom to serve and to be humble of heart in the midst of all and to give to others 'with open hands' (St Therese of Lisieux). The journey will be your part in the plan of God to enable others to begin their pilgrimage, so they too are able to evolve spiritually, and can also become a part of the kingdom of God, whilst we all walk our soul journey upon earth and towards God!

In writing the final draft for this chapter, I sat to reflect and listened to 'The Trout' composed by Schubert who died at the early age of 30. The final movement, the Allegro Gusto, a repetitive theme of music, illustrated for me, how we must live life in simple repetitiveness each day in order to form our life. Sometimes when the tedious and boring, is undertaken with love in hearts, it becomes a vehicle to enable us to journey with our everyday living – differently. It enables our ordinariness, to be transformed into something greater than what we once were, because with a new inner awareness, we respond with respect to whatever and with whomever we encounter, as opportunity to be in presence with God, to do ordinary things with extra-ordinary love in that practice of God's presence. As we have become spiritually awakened!

The practice of the presence of God was adopted by Brother Lawrence a lay Carmelite. Lawrence engaged with that presence from the encounters he had from the ordinary contact of daily living. It is within the very ordinariness of life that a sense of the sacred evolved from the encounters Lawrence had. Thich Nhat Hanh similarly explains that concept in The Miracle of Mindfulness. The ordinary everyday repetitive things of life, when practiced with mindfulness – become sacred.

The sacred we then begin to sense within our heart, arises not from mere thought but from our inner state of respectful awareness for all that is a part of life. Then we are compelled to assist others who also want, *and who need to make the soul's journey*. It is the essence of love within us that has softened our heart, to become more compassionate and kind, regardless of what religious belief or otherwise we hold. All of the world's great religions, if examined closely, are formed from the essence of universal peace, and of that need to love others. From that perspective, which is the ground of our very being, of our humanness, we are led to respect the sacred in everything and in everyone, regardless of background, creed or none, or gender. From that understanding at the end of journeying with our soul, we are held by God and become instruments of love, God's 'hands and feet' on earth (Teresa of Avila). It is our great fiat as we step out to journey once again, back to the source of life in which there is unity in God, from which a new Eden can be created in the future for our planet Earth. We thus leave our earth a better place for our being here. What else would you wish to do with your gift of valuable insightfulness now after having made that journey to your core?

We thus become co-creators and holders of the sacred flame in this life to bring to others, the love of truth and of God.

Finis

BIBLIOGRAPHY

Biblical sources are extracted from:

1. Holy Bible. 2004. *New Revised Standard Version*. Peabody MA: Hendrickson Publishers.
2. The New English Bible, Popular Edition. 1961. Oxford University Press: Cambridge.

   It is offered simply as the Bible to all who, in reading, teaching, or in worship, may care to use it. [backcover] No copyright on frontispiece.

3. St Teresa of Avila. 1995. *The Interior Castle*. Great Britain: Fount Paperbacks. Foreword by Robert Van de Weyer.

   Reflections are drawn from the inspiration of Teresa throughout this book with support from The Gospel of Matthew and Psalm 63.

4. Tillich, P. 1963. *Systematic Theology. Vol. 3*. Chicago: University of Chicago Press. (pp.231-235)
5. Kleinman, A. 1986. *Social Origins of Distress and Disease. Depression, Neurasthenia and Pain in Modern China*. New Haven & London: Yale University Press.
6. Pert, C. 2000. *Your Body is your Subconscious Mind*. Boulder: Sounds True Inc.
7. Thich Nhat Hanh. 2008. *The Miracle of Mindfulness*. UK: Random.
8. Chodron, Pema. 2001. *The Wisdom of No Escape: How to Love Yourself and Your World*. Hammersmith London: Harper Collins. (p.12)

9. Maas, Robin & O'Donnell, Gabriel. 1990. *Spiritual Traditions for the Contemporary Church*. Nashville: Abingdon. The Examen (pp. 198-200).
10. John of the Cross. *Dark Night of The Soul*. Translation by Starr, M. 2003. Riverhead Books New York.
11. Wikimedia 101 Zen sayings.
12. Maas, Robin & O'Donnell, Gabriel. 1990. *Spiritual Traditions for the Contemporary Church*. Nashville: Abingdon. Practicum 1- Reading for Holiness: Lectio Divina (pp.45-54).
13. De Meester, Conrad. 1982. *With Empty Hands: The Message of Therese of Lisieux*. Homebush, NSW: St Paul Publications. (p.46)
14. a' Kempis, Thomas. 1955. *The Imitation of Christ*. Eason & Son, LTD: Dublin.
15. Childress, James & Macquarrie, John. 1986. *The Westminster Dictionary of Christian Ethics*. Philadelphia: The Westminster Press.
16. The Divine Office. 1976. *Morning and Evening Prayer*. London: Collins. (p.1141)
17. American Psychiatric Association. 2000. *Diagnostic and Statistical Manual of Mental Illness DSM 1V–TR*. Washington, DC: Office of Publishing Operations, American Psychiatric Association.
18. Griffiths, Bede. 1976. *Return to the Centre*. U.K. Collins, Fount Paperback. (p.144).

APPENDIX 1

Lectio Divina (Guigo 11)

Set aside a time every day to read and to reflect on sacred texts, sacred wisdom that will assist you to engage with the Divine, and will lead to a transformation in your life, when practiced daily.

Opening prayer – "Lord Jesus, you who are the Son of the Living God, teach me to listen to what you tell me through the Holy Scriptures and to discover your face there" (Guigo ll). Or

Creator of all, guide me, teach me to listen to your voice, that which is deep within me, and to there discover your holiness.

The reading of the text – follow the reading you select for the day and pray each morning and evening. Select a verse, from psalm, or any other tract, or a word that you would like to reflect on. Read through, and identify the characteristics of the tract, and the key words, that draw you.

Meditation – engage with the tract. Determine what the meaning is behind it. What does God speak to me, from this? What does this teach me from my daily life? How can the knowledge bring change into my world?

Prayer – Let yourself be drawn into prayer from that reading, speak to God as if God were sitting next to you. Humbly seek God's grace, and ask how you can become a source of support from the revelation of what you have read and meditated on.

Contemplation – You sit to wait for God's response to prayer, but not in anticipation.

Action/Response – Now choose a word or phrase, bring it to your attention throughout your day and act on that, allowing it to become the focus of how you might act in your life today.

Epilogue

Many decades ago my mother and I, would journey by train into the city and disembark at Central Station from where we walked the hill to Hordens and then on to Mark Foy's. In Central Park, I saw extreme poverty for the first time – that of the physical kind – it took the form of what my mother informed me, was a 'bag lady' and there were also many vagrant and destitute men who roamed the park, where they lived at night and under the archways of the station. They would emerge early in the morning to drift off somewhere during the daytime. It saddened me, as these people appeared to have nothing, possibly after they had been stripped of all they ever had in life. Perhaps, their home, their family, friends, income and social support? Modern day lepers, shunned! In stark contrast to this, too many people have too much choice, with an excess of many commodities and consumerable items, while others have little. Despite our material abundance, many remain – soulless!

The question begs to be asked, where is poverty now to be found?

About the Author

My work life has ended after some ordinary and some extraordinary experiences were a part of a professional life. I assumed different roles over that lifetime; midwife, community nurse, and with a first degree in social sciences began academic work in 1988 at Curtin University Perth, and then taught at Edith Cowan University until 2001. I abandoned academic work to take up shift work as a clinical nurse in aged care to support myself, in order to further study for a degree in theology [Murdoch University, 2007] while concurrently undertaking a doctoral degree [Curtin University, 2012]. Aged care stimulated my concern for the spiritual wellbeing of the ageing and led to the completion of a Post Grad Dip in Ageing & Pastoral Studies [St Marks Theological College Canberra, of Charles Sturt University] in 2013. A Clinical Pastoral Education program [Gosford Chaplaincy Dept] was completed in June 2011. A new journey thus began!

Now the spiritual wellbeing of life compels me, not just for myself, but for others around me, who like me, are ageing. My journey has led to the involvement to research the spiritual wellbeing of the aged person. My soul is nourished by contemplative prayer assisted by Lectio Divina. I am a member of the Monasteries of the Heart – 'a new movement for a new world' – a secular way of living Benedictine spirituality, led by Sr. Joan Chittister, OSB, and the Benedictine Sisters of Pennsylvania, USA.

CPSIA information can be obtained
at www.ICGtesting.com
Printed in the USA
LVHW052152260622
722161LV00001B/107